Edited by Jim Heimann with
an introduction by Willy Wilkerson

The Golden Age of Advertising – the

50s

TASCHEN

KÖLN LONDON LOS ANGELES MADRID PARIS TOKYO

Jim Heimann

RICAN

The 1950s

From Poodles To Presley, Americans Enter The Atomic Age

by Jim Heimann

The atomic bomb changed everything. By 1950, Americans were slowly accepting the fact that something fundamentally different was going on in society. Despite the victories of World War II and a post-war prosperity that brought a rush of unheralded consumerism, atomic power had many Americans wondering what the future held. At the end of the summer in the year 1949, the explosion of a Russian atomic bomb confirmed that the United States was no longer the sole possessor of the mightiest nuclear device in the world and Americans responded in different ways. Some bought Geiger counters to mine for uranium. Others started digging bomb shelters in their backyards to protect them from a nuclear blast. But regardless of their action, for most Americans the advent of the bomb signaled an end to an age of innocence and a time to buy, buy, buy.

The early 1950s witnessed the continued paranoia that accompanied the possession of nuclear warheads. The U.S. government, in an attempt to keep one step ahead of the Russians, initiated an arms race. If the Reds had an atomic bomb, America needed a more powerful one. The resulting H-bomb

put the U. S. that one strategic step ahead. This rush to create the world's top nuclear power ushered in the atomic age which was quickly joined by other sobriquets for new technological developments. Soon advertising copy was peppered with references to the jet age and the space age. A new category of advertising emerged addressing the Cold War. The tanks and jeeps of World War II were replaced by nuclear subs and guided missiles. It was in this atmosphere that Madison Avenue, in attempting to put a positive spin on the atom and doomsday predictions, embraced nuclear power and applied it to advertising. The "peaceful atom" was now working for Americans. In one amazing ad, a mushroom cloud is accompanied by copy which claims that "Even this cloud has a silver lining." Advertisers appropriated space helmets and rockets to sell cereal. Car designers came up with exaggerated tail fins for automobiles to express this new accelerated speed. And the American public ate it up.

Unlike previous decades in which the Depression and World War II condoned frugality and rationing, American consumers of the 1950s were experiencing an unprecedented phenomenon. A generation born before and during the Depression were of an age where their earning power created a pocket of wealth. This, combined with a declining number of individuals to share it and the resumption of American industry's aggressive consumer economy after World War II, set the stage for a buying binge that Americans would indulge in for the foreseeable future. With a productivity rate of two percent per year between 1945 and 1955 Americans were buying 75 % of the cars and appliances on the earth. Despite the shadow of atomic obliteration hanging over the American consciousness, advertisers continued to barrage the public, a new "mass market," with products that were newer, better and faster. And Americans felt entitled to it. Striving to lead normal productive lives after saving the world from Axis aggression, the American public looked beyond their pre-

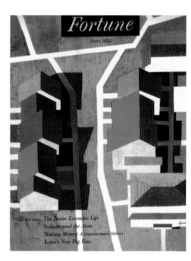

World War II days and gazed to the future – and the future looked great. At least as seen through the eyes of television, magazines and advertising.

Bolstered by the media, consumers obliged this onslaught of advertising by buying the endless array of products. Home ownership, which most Americans considered their birthright, along with disposable income were the foundation for much of this consumption in the 1950s. Prompted by post-war housing shortages, the drift away from the city and into the suburbs was well on its way by the beginning of the decade with 23.6 million Americans owning their own homes. By 1960, there were 32.8 million homeowners. This suburban trend was firmly established with the construction of sprawling suburbs such as Levittown, New York, a former potato field that was developed into a mass of 17,447 houses in 1951. With all of these detached, single family dwellings came the need to furnish and maintain them. Within ten years the sale of lawn and porch furniture sales jumped from 53.6 million dollars to 145.2 million dollars, while automatic washer sales almost doubled from 1.7 million to 2.6 million.

Striving to lead normal productive lives after saving the world from Axis aggression the American public looked beyond their pre-World War II days and gazed to the future. And the future looked great.

After home ownership, the automobile was next in line for Americans unabated consumption. The introduction of the 1955 models in the fall of 1954 set off a buying frenzy. Redesigned to reflect the era's pre-occupation with speed, the new line of cars had sleek styling and lots of chrome. Chevrolets in particular received much of the attention with their range of colors and dynamic new look. The hint of luxury was implied in marketing the cars and buyers were promised a bit of the future as well. An ad for the Ford Lincoln asked buyers "Why be tied down to yesterday?" while copy for the Buick Roadmaster suggested that everywhere you went a red carpet would be rolled out upon your arrival. The status associated with automobiles was unavoidable. Cars reflected an economic standard and a place in society for their owners. They also could be seen as reflections of their driver's personality.

As the decade progressed, the extremes of car design were taken to their limits. Fins got larger, chrome embellished almost every surface and the size of the cars expanded to near-impossible lengths. The advertising which accompanied these behemoths bordered on pretension. The doomed Ford

Edsel claimed "They'll know you've arrived when you drive up in an Edsel." The Buick Limited was "The car conceived and created to change your ideas of luxury motoring." The ad copy for the Pontiac declared "A bold new car for a bold new generation." The trend in massive cars would last into the early 1960s when smaller compact imports including the Volkswagen, an odd little German car which appeared at the end of the decade, would profoundly change the future of American car buying. Until then, America basked in an era unmatched in automobile production.

Serious consumption was joined by whimsical buying in a move that seemed to counter the harsh realities of nuclear annihilation. Americans wholeheartedly embraced a whole range of fads in the 1950s buying unnecessary objects out of sheer compulsion. Coonskin caps, chlorophyll-infused products, Capri pants, bongos, shrunken heads, hula hoops, flying saucers, Tupperware, and purple people eaters were bought with abandon. For one short period in the mid 1950s anything that was pink was in. Pink refrigerators, pink stoves, pink lipstick, pink dress shirts and pink typewriters. Ads

for GE's pink light bulbs boasted that they would flatter complexions and furnishings. Copy for Royal portable typewriters gushed that finally you had choice in the color of your typewriter. The Russian threat would just have to wait until Americans could stock up on pink toilet paper.

In the 1950s, the public was badgered to consume, and no one wanted to be old fashioned. Replacing the old with the new was considered a good thing. Advertisements reinforced the idea that to be modern was to be hip. In design and architecture, modern usually meant European Modernism. But modern also came to mean that objects were manufactured, not hand made, and most had a planned obsolescence built in. The American public trusted that industry had their best interests in mind and that they were being led to a better future by accepting everything modern. As long as things looked newer, exciting and better, consumption rolled swiftly along.

Television, the new media giant that was a plaything in the 1930s and introduced to the public in the 1940s, had become in the '50s an all-consuming monolith absorbing the attention of every man, woman and child across the country. In just five years, the sale of TV sets climbed from 3.1 million in 1950 to more than 32 million by mid-decade. Game shows, cartoons, variety shows, Westerns, cop shows and an endless variety of sit-at-home entertainment entranced American viewers night after night. Technological advances rapidly increased the size of TV sets and advertisers prompted consumers to go for the 21-inch set that was the price of the 17-inch set. Ads for Crosley televisions emphasized family viewing with "full room vision." Within a few years, this trend was reversed and sets were being downsized for portability. "The personal TV for take it with you use" was how GE advertised the new portable. By 1959, Americans were staring at the "boob tube" for an average of six hours a day, seven days a week. Its across-the-board appeal would directly compete with and disable the motion picture industry. Eventually

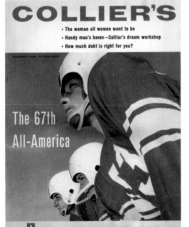

it also would erode the world of print, signaling the slow decline of American magazine advertising.

Music in the early 1950's was affected by the changing tastes of the post-war period. The slow elimination of the Big Band sound which had dominated the music world for almost two decades was replaced in the charts by a range of tunes that were a mixture of sweet vocals, ballads, a bit of hillbilly/country and mood music. Liberace, dressed in a tuxedo while playing at his candlelit grand piano, exemplified this musical malaise. Making up to a million dollars a year, he catered to these sappy tastes. Just as popular was Mitch Miller, and his *Sing Along with Mitch* albums which sold 1.75 million records in fifteen months. With the jukebox fading and replaced by the potent combination of TV, the portable record player and the compact 45-rpm record, the music scene was ripe for a change. By far the defining moment in this musical hodgepodge was the eruption of rock and roll in the mid 1950s. Led by black artists who defined the roots of rock, it was Elvis Presley who captured the attention of the huge teenage population and changed the direction of Ameri-

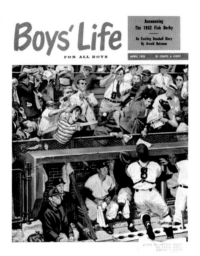

can music for generations to come. His first three singles sold over a million copies and he had amassed 120 million in record and merchandising sales by 1960. Elvis as a phenomenon was quickly followed by other teenage idols. Their popularity was boosted by TV programs such as Dick Clark's American Bandstand, the top rated teenage program that could make or break a rising star. The world of rock and roll was largely ignored by print advertisers in mass market magazines. Radio was the primary advertising conduit, though a growing number of teen and fan magazines began to fill the void.

As an antidote to the conformity portrayed on television and the reality of the blandness of suburban living, some Americans would actively challenge the norm by nonconformist behavior. In a prelude to the turbulent sixties individuals such as author Jack Kerouac would personify the anti-social behavior that became the backbone of Beat culture, providing the straight world with the Beat Generation. James Dean became the cinema version of the lonely, alienated and misunderstood youth. Juvenile delinquents were the polar opposite of the squeaky-clean football players and cheerleaders America

liked to think were the backbone of the country. Teenagers meanwhile reveled in the symbolic trappings of rebellion in an affront to their parents middle class values. Hot rods and customized cars represented the free expression of car design disengaged from Detroit's assembly line product. Jazz, which had simmered and evolved into an abstract and free form expression, perfectly matched the mood of this underground swell of new hipsters and was an alternative to the cloying pop music of the masses. These undercurrents of social change paralleled the optimistic picture painted in the advertisements of magazines and the mainstream press and anticipated the social upheaval the next decade would bring.

The '50s could be distilled into a world of pink and charcoal gray. The blandness of the man in the gray flannel suit versus the pink pouting lips of sex goddess Marilyn Monroe. The black and white McCarthy hearings and pink poodles advertising liquor. The dull conformity of the suburbs versus the wild bongo rhythms of the beatniks. The unabashed consumerism of the 1950s expressed in the advertisements of the decade reflected the extremes of a modern affluent generation and would lead Americans into the turbulent 1960s rejecting and reflecting on the tidal wave of 1950s consumerism.

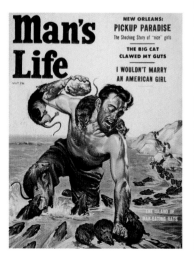

Die Fünfziger

Mit pinkfarbenen Pudeln und Presley ins Atomzeitalter

Von Jim Heimann

Cool cookery for summer • Family fun at Western beaches

Mit der Atombombe wandelte sich alles. Um 1950 akzeptierten die Amerikaner allmählich, dass sich in der Gesellschaft etwas fundamental veränderte. Ungeachtet der Siege im Zweiten Weltkrieg und einer Nachkriegsprosperität, die einen ungeahnten Konsumrausch mit sich brachte, fragten sich viele, was die Zukunft bereithalte. Durch die Explosion einer russischen Atombombe im Spätsommer 1949 bestätigte sich, dass die Vereinigten Staaten nicht länger im Alleinbesitz des stärksten Sprengkörpers der Welt waren. Und auf diese Erkenntnis reagierten die Amerikaner auf unterschiedliche Weise. Manche kauften Geigerzähler, um nach Uranvorkommen zu suchen. Andere schachteten bei sich zu Hause Luftschutzbunker aus, um sich vor einem nuklearen Sprengsatz zu schützen. Doch was auch immer sie taten: Für die meisten Amerikaner signalisierte die Bombe das Ende eines Zeitalters der Unschuld und einer Epoche des Kaufens, Kaufens, Kaufens.

Die frühen Fünfziger erlebten die fortwährende Paranoia, die mit dem Besitz nuklearer Sprengköpfe einherging. In dem Bestreben, den Russen einen Schritt voraus zu bleiben, setzte die US-Regierung ein

Wettrüsten in Gang. Wenn die Roten eine Atombombe hatten, so benötigte Amerika eine stärkere. Die daraufhin entwickelte Wasserstoffbombe brachte den USA einen Vorsprung um diesen einen strategischen Schritt. Der Kampf um die nukleare Vormachtstellung mündete in das so genannte Atomzeitalter, das bald im Zuge anderer technischer Neuentwicklungen um weitere Etikettierungen ergänzt wurde. So waren die Werbebotschaften rasch mit Anspielungen auf das Düsenzeitalter und das Weltraumzeitalter gespickt. Eine neue Kategorie von Werbung entstand, die auf den Kalten Krieg abhob. An die Stelle der Panzer und Jeeps aus dem Zweiten Weltkrieg traten Atom-U-Boote und ferngesteuerte Raketen. In diesem Klima versuchte man in der Madison Avenue, nuklearer Bedrohung und Weltuntergangsverheißungen eine positive Wendung zu geben, indem man sich die Atomenergie werbewirksam zu Eigen machte. Jetzt arbeitete das »friedliche Atom« für die Amerikaner. In einer erstaunlichen Werbung ziert einen Atompilz der Spruch: »Auch diese Wolke ist ein Silberstreif am Horizont«. Die Werbeleute bemühten Raumhelme und Raketen, um Frühstücksflocken zu verkaufen. Autodesigner warteten mit übertriebenen Heckflossen auf, um der neuen beschleunigten Geschwindigkeit Ausdruck zu verleihen. Und die amerikanische Öffentlichkeit biss an.

Anders als in früheren Jahrzehnten, in denen aufgrund der Depression oder des Zweiten Weltkriegs Sparsamkeit und Rationierung auf der Tagesordnung standen, erlebten die amerikanischen Verbraucher in den Fünfzigern ein beispielloses Phänomen. Eine Generation, die vor und während der Depression zur Welt gekommen war, war nun in einem Alter, in dem ihre Kaufkraft ein Vermögen ausmachte. In Kombination mit der abnehmenden Zahl derjenigen, die es sich teilen mussten, und der nach dem Zweiten Weltkrieg wieder einsetzenden aggressiven Konsumgüterproduktion der amerikanischen Industrie bereitete dies den Boden dafür, dass die Amerikaner auf absehbare

Zeit dem Kaufrausch frönten. Mit einer jährlichen Produktivitätssteigerung von zwei Prozent zwischen 1945 und 1955 kauften die Amerikaner 75 % der Autos und Geräte auf der ganzen Welt. Ungeachtet des Schattens atomarer Auslöschung, der auf dem amerikanischen Bewußtsein lastete, bombardierten die Werber das Publikum – einen neuen »Massenmarkt« – mit Produkten, die neuer, besser und schneller waren. Und die Amerikaner hatten nach ihrem Empfinden einen Anspruch darauf. Die USA hatten die Welt aus dem Würgegriff der Achsenmächte befreit. Im Bemühen, ein normales Leben zu führen, blickte die amerikanische Bevölkerung nun über ihre Vorkriegstage hinaus und schaute in die Zukunft. Und die sah großartig aus. Zumindest mit Blick auf das Fernsehen, auf Magazine und die Werbung.

Von den Medien ermuntert, honorierten die Verbraucher den Werbefeldzug und kauften eine nimmer endende Reihe von Produkten. Die Konsumwelle in den Fünfzigern gründete im Immobilienbesitz, den die meisten Amerikaner für ihr angeborenes Recht hielten, sowie im Anstieg des verfügbaren Einkommens. Die von der Nachkriegswohnungsnot verursachte Abwanderung aus den

Die USA hatten die Welt aus dem Würgegriff der Achsenmächte befreit. Im Bemühen, ein normales Leben zu führen, blickte die amerikanische Bevölkerung nun über ihre Vorkriegstage hinaus und schaute in die Zukunft. Und die sah großartig aus.

Innenstädten in die Vorstädte war zu Beginn des Jahrzehnts in vollem Schwange: 23,6 Millionen Amerikaner nannten ein Haus ihr Eigen. Um 1960 gab es bereits 32,8 Millionen Hausbesitzer. Endgültig etablierte sich dieser Trend zum Suburbanen mit dem Bau ausufernder Vorstädte wie Levittown, New York, ein ehemaliger Kartoffelacker, auf dem 1951 die Unmenge von 17.447 neu gebauten Häusern stand. Diese ganzen freistehenden Einfamilienheime wollten möbliert und erhalten werden. Binnen zehn Jahren stieg der Verkauf von Garten- und Terrassenmöbeln von 53,6 auf 145,2 Millionen Dollar an, während der Absatz von Waschmaschinen von 1,7 auf 2,6 Millionen Stück hochschnellte.

Nach dem Eigenheim kam im ungebremsten Konsum das Auto dran. Die Einführung der 1955er Modelle im Herbst 1954 löste ein Kauffieber aus. Im Design sollte sich jetzt die zeitgemäße Idee von Geschwindigkeit spiegeln, so dass die neue Autolinie in schnittigem Styling und mit jeder Menge Chrom daherkam. Viel Aufsehen erweckten vor allem die Chevrolets mit ihrer Farbskala und neuen dynamischen Erscheinung. Die Autowerbung winkte mit Luxus und versprach den Käufern ein Stück Zukunft. Eine Reklame für den Ford Lincoln stellte den Käufern die Frage »Warum an Gestern gefesselt bleiben?«, während die für den Buick Roadmaster suggerierte, wo immer man hinfahre, werde einem bei der Ankunft ein roter Teppich ausgerollt. An das Auto knüpfte sich unumgänglich der soziale Status. Zugleich ließ es sich als Ausdruck der Persönlichkeit seines Fahrers betrachten.

Mit Voranschreiten des Jahrzehnts drang das Autodesign an die extremsten Grenzen vor. Die Flossen wurden immer voluminöser, jede nur denkbare Fläche zierte Chrom, und die Länge der Karosserien dehnte sich ins nahezu Unmögliche. Die Werbungen für derlei Ungetüme strahlten ebenfalls etwas Vermessenes aus. Der inzwischen längst von der Bildfläche verschwundene Ford Edsel versprach: »Sie werden wissen, dass du angekommen bist, wenn du in einem Edsel vorfährst« und der Slogan für Pontiac lautete:

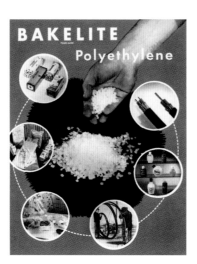

»Ein kühnes neues Auto für eine kühne neue Generation«. Der Trend zu massiven Limousinen sollte bis in die frühen Sechziger anhalten, als kleinere Importwagen auf dem Markt auftauchten und die Zukunft des Fahrzeugmarktes in Amerika in eine andere Richtung lenkten – darunter auch der sonderbare kleine Käfer aus Deutschland, der zum Ende des Jahrzehnts eingeführt wurde.

Angesichts der reellen Drohung nuklearer Vernichtung setzte man nicht mehr nur auf die sicheren Werte, sondern gab sich auch dem Lustkauf hin. Nach Herzenslust schwelgten die Amerikaner in den Fünfgern in einer ganzen Welt von Gimmicks und kauften schier zwanghaft überflüssiges Zeug. Waschbärkappen, Caprihosen, Bongos, Schrumpfköpfe, Hula-Hoop-Reifen, Fliegende Untertassen und Tupperware fanden reißenden Absatz. Für einen kurzen Zeitraum Mitte der fünfziger Jahre war alles in, was pink war: Kühlschränke, Elektroherde, Lippenstifte, Smokinghemden und Schreibmaschinen. Die Werbung für General Electric's pinkfarbene Glühbirnen behauptete vollmundig, deren Licht schmeichele dem Teint und der Wohnungseinrichtung. Der Text für Royal Reiseschreibmaschinen

schwärmte davon, endlich könne man sich die Farbe seiner Schreibmaschine selber aussuchen. Die russische Bedrohung würde einfach warten müssen, bis die Amerikaner ihre Vorräte an pinkfarbenem Toilettenpapier aufgefüllt hätten.

Unter dem allgemeinen Trommeln zum Konsum wollte in den fünfziger Jahren keiner mehr altmodisch sein. Das Alte durch das Neue zu ersetzen, galt als eine gute Sache. Die Werbungen verstärkten die Vorstellung, modern sein bedeute hip sein. In Design und Architektur wurde unter »modern« für gewöhnlich der europäische Modernismus verstanden. Doch jetzt bezeichnete »modern« auch Gegenstände, die fabrikmäßig hergestellt wurden. Die amerikanische Bevölkerung vertraute darauf, dass die Industrie ihr Bestes im Sinn habe und sie in eine bessere Zukunft führen würde, wenn sie nur alles Moderne annähme. Und solange die Dinge neuer und aufregender aussahen, wurde munter weiterkonsumiert.

Das Fernsehen, der neue Medienriese, der in den Dreißigern noch ein Spielzeug gewesen war und in den Vierzigern an die Öffentlichkeit gebracht wurde, war in den Fünfzigern zu einem Monolithen geworden,

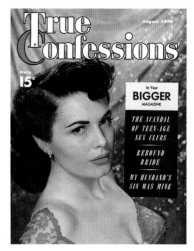

der die Aufmerksamkeit sämtlicher Männer, Frauen und Kinder im Lande okkupierte. In fünf Jahren kletterte der Verkauf von Fernsehgeräten von 3,1 Millionen auf über 32 Millionen im Jahr 1955. Spieleshows, Zeichentrickfilme, Sketchsendungen, Western, Polizeiserien und ein endloses Allerlei an Pantoffelunterhaltung berieselten Abend für Abend die amerikanische Zuschauerschaft. Technische Fortschritte ließen die Fernsehgeräte rasch größer werden, und die Werber bewogen die Verbraucher, sich zum Preis des 17-Zollers den 21-Zoll-Apparat zuzulegen. Die Werbung für Crosley Fernsehgeräte betonte das Betrachten im Familienkreis bei »raumfüllender Sicht«. Binnen weniger Jahre kehrte sich dieser Trend um, und die Geräte wurden der Tragbarkeit halber verkleinert. »Dein persönliches TV zum Mitnehmen«, bewarb General Electric den neuen Tragbaren. Um 1959 starrten die Amerikaner durchschnittlich sechs Stunden pro Tag in die »Glotze«, und zwar an sieben Tagen die Woche. Der breitenwirksame Reiz des Fernsehens sollte unmittelbar mit der Filmindustrie konkurrieren und diese schließlich aus dem Rennen werfen. Das Fernsehen begann auch das Verlagswesen zu schwächen und den Niedergang der amerikanischen Magazinwerbung einzuläuten.

Auf die Musik der frühen fünfziger Jahre wirkten sich die gewandelten Geschmäcker der Nachkriegszeit aus. Der Big-Band-Sound, der in der Musik fast zwei Jahrzehnte lang den Ton angegeben hatte, verklang allmählich und wich in den Charts einem Strauß bunter Melodien, in dem sich süßlicher Gesang, Balladen, ein bisschen Hillbilly oder Country mit »Stimmungsmusik« mischte. Liberace, im Smoking am kerzenbeleuchteten Flügel spielend, verkörperte diese musikalische Malaise. Bei einem Jahresverdienst von bis zu einer Million Dollar bediente er schwelgerische Gemüter. Ebenso populär waren Mitch Miller und seine Alben *Sing Along with Mitch*, von denen in 15 Monaten 1,75 Millionen Aufnahmen verkauft wurden. Als die Jukebox gegenüber der wirkungsmächtigen Kombination von Fernseher, trag-

barem Plattenspieler und 45er-Scheiben ins Hintertreffen geriet, war die Musikszene reif für eine Veränderung. Am folgenreichsten war natürlich der Ausbruch des Rock and Roll in den Mittfünfzigern. Im Gefolge schwarzer Künstler, die die Wurzeln des Rock gelegt hatten, war es Elvis Presley, der das breite Teenagervolk für sich gewann und der amerikanischen Musik auf Generationen hinaus eine neue Richtung wies. Von seinen ersten drei Singles wurden über eine Million Exemplare abgesetzt, und 1960 hatte er mit dem

Verkauf von Schallplatten und Fanartikeln 120 Millionen Dollar eingefahren. Rasch folgten dem Phänomen Elvis weitere Teenageridole. Ihre Popularität wurde von Fernsehprogrammen wie Dick Clarks *American Bandstand* angekurbelt, dem meistgesehenen Teenagerprogramm, das ein aufgehendes Sternchen auch sogleich zum Verglühen bringen konnte. Die Welt des Rock and Roll wurde von den Printwerbern weitgehend ignoriert. Wichtigster Werbekanal war das Radio, wiewohl eine wachsende Zahl von Teen- und Fanmagazinen die Lücke zu füllen begann.

Als Gegengift zur Konformität, die das Fernsehen zeichnete, und zur farblosen Realität des Vorstadtlebens machten sich einige Amerikaner daran, die Norm durch ungebührliches Betragen aktiv herauszufordern. In einem Vorspiel zu den turbulenten Sechzigern verkörperte ein Autor wie Jack Kerouac das antisoziale Verhalten, das zum Leitfaden der Beatkultur wurde. James Dean war die Kinoversion der einsamen, entfremdeten und unverstandenen Jugend. Jugendliche Straftäter bildeten das Gegenmodell zu den adretten Footballspielern und Cheerleadern, in denen Amerika gerne das Rückgrat der Nation sah. Unterdessen hoben die Teenager im Ansturm gegen die Werte ihrer Eltern die symbolischen Zeichen der Rebellion aufs Panier. Heiße Öfen und umfrisierte Autos standen für einen freien Ausdruck des Fahrzeugdesigns, das sich vom Fließbandprodukt aus Detroit emanzipierte. Der Jazz, der sich in einem gehörigen Gärprozess zur abstrakten, freien Ausdrucksform entwickelt hatte, traf genau die Stimmung dieser neuen Hipster und bot eine Alternative zur abgedroschenen Popmusik der Massen. Solche zeitgleich zu dem optimistischen Mainstream vorhandenen Unterströmungen gesellschaftlicher Verhältnisse wiesen auf die sozialen Bewegungen und Unruhen voraus, die das nächste Jahrzehnt verhieß.

In einem Bild von der Lebenswelt der Fünfziger müssten Pink und Mausgrau in Kontrast gesetzt werden. Die Farblosigkeit des Herrn im grauen Flanellanzug gegen den rosaroten Schmollmund der Sexgöttin Marilyn Monroe. Die schwarzweißen McCarthy-Anhörungen gegen den pinkfarbenen Pudel, der für Likör wirbt. Die dumpfe Eintönigkeit der Vorstädte gegen die wilden Bongorhythmen der Beatniks. Der grenzenlose Konsumwahn, der sich in der Werbung dieses Jahrzehnts ausdrückt, spiegelt die Extreme einer modernen wohlhabenden Generation, die die Amerikaner in die turbulenten Sechziger führen sollte, in denen solch ungebremste Konsumbegeisterung zurückgewiesen und kritisch beleuchtet wurde.

Les Années 50

Elvis et petits caniches roses : les Américains entrent dans l'ère atomique

de Jim Heimann

La bombe atomique a tout changé. Vers 1950, les Américains se font lentement à l'idée qu'un changement fondamental se produit dans leur société. Malgré les victoires de la Seconde Guerre mondiale et une prospérité qui entraîne le pays dans un consumérisme sans précédent, le danger atomique pousse nombre d'Américains à s'interroger sur l'avenir. A la fin de l'été 1949, l'explosion d'une bombe atomique russe confirme que les Etats-Unis ne sont plus l'unique détenteur du dispositif nucléaire le plus puissant du monde. Les habitants réagissent de différentes manières. Certains se munissent de compteurs Geiger pour faire de la prospection d'uranium. D'autres se mettent à creuser des abris anti-atomiques au fond de leur jardin. Mais indépendamment de ces actions, pour la plupart des Américains l'arrivée de la bombe annonce la fin de l'innocence et la venue d'une époque où chacun ne pense plus qu'à acheter, acheter, encore acheter.

Le début des années 50 témoigne de cette paranoïa qui monte avec la propagation des ogives nucléaires. Afin de garder l'avantage sur les Russes, le gouvernement américain se lance dans la course aux armements. Si les Rouges possèdent une bombe atomique, l'Amérique doit en avoir une encore plus puissante. Le résultat, c'est la bombe H et une avance stratégique pour les USA. Cette obsession à devenir la première puissance nucléaire donne naissance au terme d'ère atomique, ainsi qu'à d'autres sobriquets accompagnant les avancées technologiques successives. Très vite, les affiches publicitaires s'émaillent de références à l'ère des supersoniques, à celle de l'espace. D'autres s'inspirent de la guerre froide. Les tanks et les Jeeps de la dernière guerre sont remplacés par des sous-marins nucléaires et des missiles téléguidés. C'est dans cette atmosphère que Madison Avenue, pour tenter d'insuffler un tour positif aux prédictions catastrophiques concernant l'atome, s'empare de l'énergie nucléaire et la lance dans la publicité. « L'atome de la paix » travaille dorénavant pour les Américains. Sur une

réclame étonnante, un champignon nucléaire est accompagné d'une légende affirmant que « même ce nuage possède un manteau d'argent ». Les annonceurs s'approprient casques d'astronautes et fusées spatiales pour vendre des céréales. Les fabricants de voitures les dotent d'ailerons fuselés qui s'inspirent de cette vitesse fantastique. Le public américain est aux anges.

Contrairement aux décennies précédentes, où la Crise de 29 puis la Seconde Guerre mondiale avaient imposé frugalité et rationnement, les consommateurs des années 50 vivent un phénomène sans précédent. Une génération née avant et pendant la Crise a atteint l'âge où son pouvoir d'achat la place en position de richesse. Ce phénomène, le fait qu'un nombre moindre d'individus y participe, et l'extraordinaire reprise économique de l'industrie américaine après la guerre, incitent les Américains à dépenser sans compter. Avec un taux de productivité de deux pour cent par an, entre 1945 et 1955, ils achètent 75% des voitures et des appareils fabriqués sur la terre. Ignorant l'inquiétude nucléaire qui plane, les annonceurs continuent d'inonder le public, nouveau « marché de grande distribution », de

WESTWAYS
SEPTEMBER, 1955   20 CENTS

MOTORING UNDER THE ARC
OF THE FABULOUS SOUTHWEST

A GUIDE TO THE RECREATIONAL
AND SCENIC AREAS OF AMERICA'S NEVER-NEVER LAND

produits toujours plus nouveaux, plus pratiques et plus rapides. Et les Américains pensent qu'ils l'ont bien mérité. Les Etats-Unis avaient sauvé le monde du déluge de feu et de cendres. S'efforçant de reprendre une vie normale, la population américaine voulait oublier la guerre et regardait à présent vers l'avenir. Un avenir qui s'annonçait formidable.

Du moins vu à travers le regard de la télévision, des magazines et de la publicité. Encouragés par les médias, les consommateurs obéissent à ces attaques publicitaires et achètent tout ce qui leur est incessamment proposé. Devenir propriétaire, ce que la plupart des Américains considèrent comme un droit, et jouir de revenus disponibles, tels sont les principaux axes de la consommation des années 50. Conséquence du manque de logements après la guerre, s'éloigner de la ville en direction de la banlieue s'inscrit alors comme réalité sociale et 23,6 millions d'Américains deviennent propriétaires de leur domicile. En 1960, ils sont 32,8 millions. Cette migration entraîne la construction de banlieues interminables telles que Levittown, New York, ancien champ de pommes de terre, qui en 1951, se couvre de 17 447 maisons. Tous ces pavillons individuels, il faut les meubler et les maintenir en bon état. Dans les dix ans qui suivent, la vente de meubles de jardin et de véranda passe de 53,6 à 145,2 millions de dollars. Celle des machines à laver automatiques double presque, passant de 1,7 à 2,6 millions.

Après l'acquisition du logement, l'automobile occupe la deuxième place dans cette consommation constante des Américains. La mise en vente des modèles 1955, à l'automne 1954, provoque une véritable frénésie. Redessinées pour refléter le désir de vitesse de l'époque, ces voitures arborent des lignes fuselées et se parent de chromes. Les Chevrolet suscitent un intérêt particulier par leur gamme de couleurs et leur allure dynamique. Pour la commercialisation, on parle aux acheteurs de luxe et d'avenir. Une publicité pour la Ford Lincoln leur pose la question : « Pourquoi rester attaché au

Les Etats-Unis avaient sauvé le monde du déluge de feu et de cendres. S'efforçant de reprendre une vie normale, la population américaine voulait oublier la guerre et regardait à présent vers l'avenir. Un avenir qui s'annonçait formidable.

passé ? », tandis que celle de la Buick Road-master vous assure que, où que vous alliez, on déroulera le tapis rouge, rien que pour vous. Impossible d'éviter la relation entre automobile et statut social. La voiture reflète le niveau économique et financier de son propriétaire. Elle est sans doute aussi l'écho de sa personnalité.

A mesure que la décennie avance, toutes les possibilités du design sont explorées. Les ailerons se gonflent, le chrome vient souligner presque chaque surface et la taille des voitures atteint des longueurs à la limite du possible. La publicité qui accompagne ces mastodontes n'est pas sans prétention. La malheureuse Ford Edsel proclame : « Ils sauront que c'est vous, quand vous arriverez dans votre Edsel ». La Buick Limited s'affirme « la voiture conçue et créée pour changer vos idées en matière de luxe ». La Pontiac enfin se déclare « une voiture intrépide pour une génération qui l'est tout autant ». Ce goût pour la voiture massive va se perpétuer jusqu'au début des années soixante, où l'importation de modèles compacts comme la Volkswagen, petite allemande apparue à la fin de la décennie, viendra profondément

changer les perspectives des acheteurs américains. Jusque-là, en ce qui concerne la production automobile, l'Amérique profite d'un succès inégalé.

Cette consommation sérieuse s'accompagne d'un goût pour les achats de fantaisie, sans doute en réponse à l'angoisse d'une catastrophe nucléaire. Dans les années 50, les Américains s'adonnent à toute une série d'engouements qui les poussent irrépressiblement à acheter des choses parfaitement inutiles. Ils dépensent sans compter pour des casquettes en peau de raton-laveur, des produits à la chlorophylle, des pantalons Toréadors, des bongos, des têtes Jivaros, des hula-hoops, des soucoupes volantes, des Tupperware, et autres mangeurs de têtes. Vers 1955, pendant une courte période, tout ce qui est rose est à la mode. Réfrigérateurs roses, fourneaux roses, rouges à lèvres roses, chemises roses et machines à écrire roses. Des publicités soutiennent que les ampoules roses de la General Electric mettent en valeur le teint et l'ameublement. Celles pour les machines à écrire portatives Royal stipulent que le choix de la couleur vous revient. La menace russe devra attendre que les Américains aient le temps de stocker leur papier toilette rose.

Dans ces années ivres de consommation, personne n'oserait se laisser dépasser par la mode. Il faut à tout prix remplacer le vieux par le neuf. La publicité renforce l'idée qu'être moderne, c'est être à la page. En matière de design et d'architecture, il n'est de Modernisme qu'européen. Mais ne sont modernes que les objets manufacturés, et non fabriqués à la main, dont la plupart sont conçus avec une obsolescence calculée. Le public américain est persuadé que la production industrielle est animée des meilleures intentions, comme de leur ouvrir la voie vers un monde meilleur, à condition d'accepter tout ce qui est moderne. Aussi longtemps que les choses semblent nouvelles, étonnantes et meilleures, la consommation a le vent en poupe.

La télévision, media gigantesque, gadget

des années 30 introduit au public dans les années 40, devient au cours des années cinquante un monolithe qui absorbe l'attention de tous, hommes, femmes et enfants, d'un bout à l'autre du pays. En cinq ans, la vente des postes passe de 3,1 millions en 1950 à plus de 32 millions vers 1955. Jeux télévisés, dessins animés, variétés, westerns, films policiers, toute une gamme de divertissements à consommer chez soi captive chaque soir l'attention d'innombrables spectateurs. Très vite, le progrès technologique agrandit la taille des écrans et les annonceurs incitent les consommateurs à acquérir un 55 cm pour le prix d'un 44 cm. Pour les télévisions Crosley, la publicité insiste sur la vie de famille avec « un écran visible de toute la pièce ». Quelques années plus tard, cette tendance s'inverse au profit de la TV petit format, donc transportable. « Une TV personnelle, pour votre seul usage », propose la General Electric. Vers 1959, les Américains regardent « la télé » en moyenne six heures par jour, sept jours par semaine. Cette attirance sans limite est une concurrence directe pour l'industrie cinématographique qu'elle met en difficulté. De plus, elle représente un danger pour la

presse écrite, et l'on note un certain déclin de la publicité dans les magazines.

La musique aussi, au début des années 50, connaît une évolution dans les goûts. Les grands orchestres qui avaient régné sur le monde de la musique pendant presque deux décennies sont lentement éliminés par toutes sortes de compositions mêlant douces mélodies, ballades, hillbilly/country et « musique d'ambiance ». Liberace, en smoking, jouant sur son piano à queue éclairé d'une bougie, illustre bien ce malaise musical. Gagnant jusqu'à un million de dollars par an, il satisfait ce goût de niaiseries. Mitch Miller est tout aussi populaire et ses albums Sing Along with Mitch (Chantez avec Mitch) se vendent à 1,75 millions d'exemplaires en quinze mois. Le juke-box perd du terrain. Il est remplacé par la combinaison TV, tourne-disque portatif et disque compact 45 tours. Ainsi paré, le monde de la musique est prêt au changement. A l'évidence, dans tout ce fatras, le moment décisif est l'irruption du rock vers le milieu des années 50. Précédé par les artistes noirs qui en définissent les racines, c'est Elvis Presley qui séduit une énorme masse d'adolescents et donne une nouvelle orientation à la musique américaine pour des générations à venir. Ses trois premiers singles se vendent à plus d'un million d'exemplaires. En 1960, il a amassé 120 millions de dollars en vente de disques et de produits dérivés. Le phénomène qu'il représente est rapidement suivi par d'autres idoles des jeunes. Leur popularité est amplifiée par des programmes télévisés comme l'American Bandstand de Dick Clark, le programme pour jeunes le plus regardé, capable de fabriquer ou de briser une carrière. Dans la presse écrite grand public, le monde du rock est largement ignoré par les annonceurs. La radio est le principal canal publicitaire, même si un nombre croissant de magazines destinés aux jeunes et aux fans commence à occuper l'espace.

En guise d'antidote au conformisme tel qu'il apparaît à la télévision et à la réalité terne de la banlieue, certains Américains cherchent à défier la norme et adoptent un comportement anticonformiste. En prélude aux turbulentes années 60, des gens comme l'écrivain Jack Kerouac représentent déjà le comportement antisocial qui va s'inscrire au centre de la culture Beat, et choquer la petite bourgeoisie. James Dean incarne la version cinématographique de la jeunesse qui se sent isolée, aliénée et incomprise. Les délinquants sont à l'opposé des joueurs de foot et des cheerleaders propres sur eux que les Américains aiment à considérer comme les représentants typiques de leur pays. Pendant ce temps, les adolescents affichent avec délectation les signes extérieurs de la rébellion et s'opposent aux valeurs petites-bourgeoises de leurs parents. Les moteurs gonflés et les voitures personnalisées manifestent une grande liberté par rapport à ce qui se pratique à Detroit, sur les chaînes de montage. Le jazz, qui a longtemps couvé avant de se transformer en une expression libre et abstraite, rassemble parfaitement les tendances underground de ces nouveaux jeunes à la coule et propose une alternative à la fade musique pop des masses. Ces courants sous-jacents se développent parallèlement à l'image optimiste renvoyée par la publicité des magazines et de la presse grand public. Ils sont les signes avant-coureurs de la dégradation et du bouleversement social qui vont marquer la décennie suivante.

Les années 50s pourraient se distiller en un monde rose et gris charbon. L'inconsistance de l'homme en costume flanelle gris opposée aux lèvres sensuelles du sex-symbol Marilyn Monroe. Les auditions en noir et blanc des procès maccarthistes, face aux caniches roses vantant des boissons alcoolisées. Le triste conformisme des banlieues opposé aux rythmes endiablés du bongo sous les doigts des Beatniks. Le consumérisme sans vergogne des années 50 qui s'exprime dans la publicité reflète les extrêmes de cette génération de l'abondance qui, pendant les années 60, allaient amener les Américains à rejeter et à repenser cette marée de consumérisme qui avait submergé les années 50.

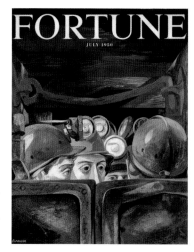

Los años cincuenta

De los caniches rosas a Elvis Presley, los estadounidenses en la era atómica

por Jim Heimann

La bomba atómica lo alteró todo. En 1950, los americanos empezaban a aceptar que se estaba produciendo un cambio sustancial en la sociedad. Pese a haber vencido en la Segunda Guerra Mundial y gozar de una prosperidad que propició un consumismo imprevisible, la existencia de armas atómicas llevaba a muchos estadounidenses a plantearse qué depararía el futuro. A finales del verano de 1949, la explosión de una bomba atómica rusa confirmó que Estados Unidos no era el único poseedor del arma nuclear más potente del mundo, lo cual suscitó reacciones de todo tipo entre la población. Algunos adquirieron contadores Geiger para buscar uranio; otros empezaron a cavar refugios atómicos en los patios traseros de sus casas para protegerse de posibles ataques nucleares. Sin embargo, al margen de cuál fuera su reacción, para la gran mayoría de los estadounidenses la existencia de la bomba atómica ponía fin a una era de inocencia y daba comienzo a una época de consumismo desenfrenado.

A principios de los años cincuenta, Estados Unidos presenció la expansión de la paranoia provocada por la posesión de cabezas nucleares. En un intento por ganar ventaja a la URSS, el gobierno estadounidense inició una carrera armamentística. Si los Rojos poseían una bomba atómica, Estados Unidos debía hacerse con un arma aún más potente, y la bomba de hidrógeno le situó a la cabeza de la carrera. La obsesión por convertirse en la primera potencia nuclear originó la aparición del término «era atómica», que pronto se vio acompañado por otros sobrenombres bajo los que se camuflaban nuevos avances tecnológicos. En breve, la publicidad impresa se vio invadida por referencias a la era de la conquista del aire y el espacio. Surgió así una nueva clase de anuncios, cuyo tema era la Guerra Fría. Los tanques y jeeps de la Segunda Guerra Mundial fueron sustituidos por submarinos nucleares y misiles teledirigidos. En medio de este clima, Madison Avenue, en un intento por transmitir cierto optimismo y despejar los augurios de la llegada del fin del

mundo, usó el poder atómico como recurso publicitario. En un sorprendente anuncio, sobre un hongo atómico aparecía el lema «Vestimos de plata el horizonte». Los publicistas utilizaron cascos espaciales y cohetes para vender cereales, los diseñadores de automóviles dotaron de alerones aerodinámicos a sus modelos... y el público norteamericano cayó rendido a sus pies.

A diferencia de lo ocurrido en las décadas precedentes, en las que la Depresión y la Segunda Guerra Mundial obligaron a la frugalidad y el racionamiento, los consumidores estadounidenses de los años cincuenta experimentaban un fenómeno sin precedentes. La generación nacida antes y durante la Depresión contaba entonces con una edad en la que la solvencia económica la colocaba en una posición privilegiada. Este hecho, junto a la supresión de las ayudas a la causa bélica, la formidable recuperación de la industria norteamericana tras la guerra y el estallido de un consumismo feroz, preparó el escenario para la orgía consumista en la que los norteamericanos se sumirían en un futuro inmediato. Con una tasa de productividad del 2 por ciento anual entre 1945 y 1955, los estadounidenses compraban el 75

por ciento de los automóviles y los electrodomésticos que se fabricaban en todo el planeta. Pese a que la sombra de la destrucción atómica se cernía sobre las conciencias americanas, los creativos continuaron bombardeando al gran público, el nuevo «mercado de masas», con productos cada vez más innovadores, rápidos y eficaces. En su lucha por llevar una vida normal y productiva tras haber salvado al mundo de la agresión de las potencias del Eje, los estadounidenses olvidaron lo acontecido antes de la Segunda Guerra Mundial y se prepararon para adentrarse en el futuro maravilloso que anunciaban la televisión, las revistas y la publicidad. Así, los consumidores se dejaron embaucar por la avalancha publicitaria y se lanzaron a comprar un sinfín de productos. Las casas de propiedad, junto con el incremento de los ingresos, constituyeron la base del consumo de los años cincuenta. La escasez de viviendas tras la guerra propició que, a principios de la década, se iniciara un movimiento migratorio de las ciudades a los barrios periféricos. En aquellas fechas, 23,6 millones de estadounidenses poseían ya una casa de propiedad; en 1960, la cifra había ascendido a 32,8 millones. La tendencia a instalarse en las zonas residenciales quedó firmemente consolidada con la edificación descontrolada de barrios como Levittown, en Nueva York, un antiguo campo de cultivo de patatas en el que, en 1951, se erigieron 17.447 viviendas. Tal cantidad de casas unifamiliares conllevó la necesidad de amueblarlas y conservarlas en buen estado. En menos de diez años, la venta de césped y mobiliario para jardines pasó de 53,6 a 145,2 millones de dólares, mientras que la cifra de lavadoras vendidas casi llegó a duplicarse (de 1,7 a 2,6 millones).

Tras la vivienda, el automóvil era el segundo bien de propiedad más preciado por los estadounidenses. La presentación de los modelos de 1955 en otoño de 1954 propició un consumo frenético. Los nuevos diseños, reflejo del entusiasmo de la época por la velocidad, presentaban líneas elegantes y multitud de adornos cromados. Los publi-

Tras salvar al mundo de la amenaza de las potencias del Eje, los estadounidenses intentaron retomar su vida cotidiana y olvidar la guerra, mientras miraban con optimismo hacia un futuro que parecía perfecto.

cistas utilizaron el lujo y el futuro prometedor como anzuelo para pescar nuevos consumidores. Un anuncio de Ford Lincoln planteaba «¿Por qué seguir anclados en el pasado?», mientras que el de Buick Roadmaster sugería al público que, allá donde viajara, una alfombra roja se desplegaría para darle la bienvenida. El estatus que se asociaba a los automóviles era obvio: constituían un símbolo de posición social y bienestar económico. Y, además, se presentaban como un reflejo de la personalidad de cada conductor.

A medida que la década avanzaba, el diseño de automóviles alcanzó su máxima expresión. Los alerones se alargaron, el cromo embelleció cada vez más superficies y las dimensiones de los vehículos se ampliaron hasta alcanzar longitudes casi imposibles. La publicidad que acompañaba a estos mastodontes rozaba la pretensión. El malhadado Ford Edsel proclamaba «Si conduce un Edsel, los demás sabrán que ha llegado». Buick Limited, por su parte, acuñó el lema «El automóvil concebido y creado para cambiar su concepción del lujo». Esta tendencia a fabricar vehículos gigantescos perduró hasta finales de los años sesenta,

cuando la importación de automóviles más compactos —entre ellos el Volkswagen, un extraño coche alemán aparecido a finales de la década— preparó el terreno para el profundo cambio que experimentaría la industria automovilística norteamericana. Hasta entonces, Estados Unidos disfrutó de una producción de automóviles jamás igualada.

El consumo descontrolado favoreció la compra de objetos fantásticos, con los cuales parecía hacerse frente a la cruda realidad de la aniquilación nuclear. Los norteamericanos abrazaron incondicionalmente toda una serie de modas pasajeras que, durante los años cincuenta, los llevaron a comprar objetos innecesarios compulsivamente. Desde sombreros de piel de mapache, hasta productos con clorofila, pasando por pantalones bombachos, bongos, cabezas reducidas, *hula-hoops*, platillos volantes y Tupperwares, todo valía para el voraz público consumidor. Durante un breve espacio de tiempo, a mediados de los años cincuenta, el rosa se convirtió en el color imperante. Todo se tiñó de rosa: los frigoríficos, las cocinas, las barras de labios, las camisas de frac y las máquinas de escribir. Los anuncios de bombillas rosas de General Electric anunciaban que su luz

realzaba el mobiliario y favorecía a las personas. La amenaza rusa tendría que esperar a que los estadounidenses pudieran almacenar papel higiénico de color rosa.

A lo largo de los años cincuenta se urgió al público a consumir y a no quedarse anticuado. La renovación de los objetos se consideraba algo positivo. Los anuncios reforzaban la idea de que ser moderno equivalía a estar al día. En los campos del diseño y la arquitectura, el término «moderno» se asimilaba al Movimiento Moderno europeo. Sin embargo, «moderno» también quería decir que los productos se fabricaban industrialmente, no a mano, y que la vida de muchos de ellos estaba previsto que fuera efímera. El público estadounidense confiaba en que la industria buscaba satisfacer sus intereses, por lo que se dejaba llevar hacia el futuro aceptando sin más todo aquello que se consideraba moderno. Siempre que los objetos parecieran innovadores, asombrosos o eficaces, su venta estaba asegurada.

La televisión, el nuevo gigante de los medios de comunicación, tras ser un mero juguete en los años treinta y difundirse entre el gran público en los años cuarenta, se había convertido en la década de los cincuenta en el monolito del consumo e hipnotizaba a hombres, mujeres y niños a lo largo y ancho del país. En tan sólo cinco años, la venta de televisores había pasado de 3,1 millones en 1950 a más de 32 millones a mediados de la década. Concursos televisivos, dibujos animados, programas de variedades, películas del oeste, filmes policíacos y una lista sin fin de entretenimientos para ver en casa embaucaban a los espectadores estadounidenses noche tras noche. Los avances tecnológicos aumentaron rápidamente las dimensiones de los televisores y se invitó a la población a adquirir una pantalla de 21 pulgadas al precio de una de 17. Los anuncios de televisores Crosley ofrecían a la familia una «Pantalla visible desde todos los ángulos». En pocos años, la tendencia se invirtió y las dimensiones de los televisores se redujeron para ofrecer una mayor facilidad de transporte. General Electric vendía sus nuevos modelos con el eslogan: «La tele personal que le acompaña a todas partes». En 1959, los norteamericanos pasaban una media de seis horas al día, siete días a la semana, postrados ante la «caja tonta». Este atractivo general no sólo supuso una férrea competencia para la industria del cine, sino que incluso se temió que la aniquilara. También entrañaba peligro para la prensa escrita, de cuyas páginas fueron desapareciendo los anuncios publicitarios.

La música de principios de los años cincuenta acusaba la influencia de los nuevos gustos emergidos tras la guerra. El sonido de las grandes orquestas, que había dominado la esfera musical durante cerca de dos décadas, fue desvaneciéndose paulatinamente de las listas de ventas para dar paso a unas melodías en las que se combinaban voces suaves, baladas, country y música ambiental. Sentado al piano con un traje chaqueta e iluminado por la luz de las velas, Liberace se convirtió en el mayor exponente de esta insulsez musical; la satisfacción de los gustos ñoños de la época le reportó unos ingresos de un millón de dólares anuales. También Mitch Miller gozaba de gran popularidad; su disco *Sing Along with Mitch* vendió 1,75 millones de ejemplares en tan sólo quince meses. Con la desaparición de las gramolas y la emergencia del televisor, el tocadiscos portátil y los discos compactos de 45 rpm, la escena musical estaba lista para experimentar un gran cambio. Y sin lugar a dudas, el momento definitivo fue la irrupción del *rock and roll* a mediados de los años cincuenta. Influido por los artistas negros que definieron las raíces del rock, Elvis Presley sedujo a la juventud y cambió el destino de la música norteamericana de las generaciones venideras. De sus primeros tres sencillos se vendieron más de un millón de copias; en 1960, las ventas de discos y *merchandising* le habían permitido amasar una fortuna de 120 millones de dólares. El fenómeno de Elvis impulsó la aparición de otros ídolos de adolescentes, cuya popularidad se acunaba en los programas televisivos, entre los que destacaba *American Bandstand*,

el programa más popular entre los jóvenes, capaz de crear o hundir a una estrella. Las revistas dirigidas al gran público apenas se hicieron eco del fenómeno del *rock and roll:* la radio fue el principal medio de transmisión hasta que una serie de revistas para adolescentes y fans vino a llenar aquel vacío. Como antídoto contra la conformidad vendida a través de la televisión y la insulsa vida en los barrios residenciales, algunos estadounidenses desafiaron las reglas haciendo halago de un comportamiento inconformista. En el preludio de los turbulentos años sesenta, individuos como el escritor Jack Kerouac personificaron el comportamiento antisocial que caracterizó la cultura Beat y la enfrentó a la clase media. James Dean se convirtió en la versión cinematográfica del joven solitario, alienado e incomprendido. Los delincuentes juveniles eran el polo opuesto a los saludables jugadores de rugby y las animadoras que los estadounidenses gustaban considerar el ejemplo de la juventud de su país. Entre tanto, los adolescentes de clase media se deleitaban rebelándose contra los valores convencionales de sus padres. Los motores trucados y los coches personalizados representaron la expresión

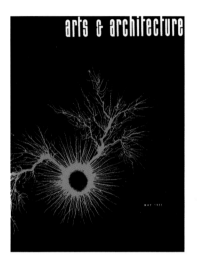

libre del diseño de automóviles alejado de las cadenas de producción en serie de Detroit. El jazz, que había ido fermentando y evolucionando hasta devenir una forma de expresión libre y abstracta, encajaba perfectamente en aquella maraña de jóvenes *underground* y se alzó como la alternativa a la empalagosa música pop comercial de la época. Las corrientes subterráneas del cambio social corrían paralelas a la imagen optimista retratada en los anuncios de las revistas y anticipaban la agitación social que protagonizaría la siguiente generación.

Los años cincuenta podrían destilarse en un mundo de color gris y rosa: la insulsez del hombre de traje de franela gris frente a los sensuales labios rosas de Marilyn Monroe; las escuchas en blanco y negro de McCarthy frente a los caniches rosas de los anuncios de licor; o la conformidad ciega de los barrios residenciales frente a los salvajes ritmos de los bongos que movieron a los *beatniks*. El consumismo desmedido de los cincuenta que reflejan los anuncios de la época retrataba los extremos de una nueva generación que conduciría a Estados Unidos a los turbulentos años sesenta y detendría la marea consumista de la década precedente.

Alcohol &
Tobacco
16

Greetings

LUCKY STRIKE
"IT'S TOASTED"

Nationally famous for good taste

On the quiet California desert before a flickering camp-fire, in historic restaurants of New Orleans, in homes across the nation, extra-dry Goebel Beer is enjoyed by those who want beer that is *first* in flavor, *first* in quality.

GOEBEL BEER
it's Mello-ized

BREWSTER

In export bottles and cans, quarts, and famous Bantam bottles and cans.

Refreshingly yours
from the land of sky blue waters!

Isn't this a cool, refreshing idea? . . . a frosty-cold glass of Hamm's beer, from the enchanted land of sky blue waters! Hamm's crisp, clean-cut taste is your kind of flavor . . . try it! Tonight!

Hamm's Beer, 1955

"Blatz is Milwaukee's Finest Beer...

It's Milwaukee's favorite beer.
I'm from Milwaukee,
I ought to know!"

says *Liberace*

Famed Milwaukee-born piano virtuoso
Columbia recording artist

• "Milwaukee is my home town," says Liberace, shown here with his valuable collection of one-of-a-kind piano miniatures. "Many people I meet on tour are surprised to learn that Blatz, in Milwaukee, outsells every other brand by a wide margin!"

• "Blatz tastes so good it's Milwaukee's favorite beer. That's quite a testimonial coming from the people living right in the beer capital of America. Make your next glass of beer *Blatz*. You'll find it everywhere. It'll be *your* favorite, too."

Today, taste  Milwaukee's finest beer!

© 1952, Blatz Brewing Co., Est. 1851 in Milwaukee, Wis.

"*My beer is* *Rheingold* —the *Dry* beer!"

says MADELYN DARROW
MISS RHEINGOLD 1958

MISS RHEINGOLD PHOTOGRAPHED WITH BMW ISETTA "300" BY PAUL HESSE · COSTUME BY BERNARD NEWMAN OF BERGDORF GOODMAN

Rheingold
EXTRA DRY
Lager Beer

It's beer as beer should taste!

Always refreshing – never filling

Seasons change, but never Rheingold Extra Dry. For Rheingold's *real-beer* taste never changes. Every glass of Rheingold is always the same. The same refreshing dryness, never sweet, never bitter, makes Rheingold New York's largest-selling beer—year after year.

Rheingold Beer, 1958

World's largest selling beer

Schlitz

THE BEER THAT MADE
MILWAUKEE FAMOUS

So Light, So Refreshing

Once more, America has paid its highest tribute to the matchless quality of Schlitz Beer. During the past year, Schlitz again led all the nation's breweries in sales. Throughout the world, people enjoyed more bottles and cans of Schlitz – *millions more* – than any other beer, at any price.

©1956 – Jos. Schlitz Brewing Company, Milwaukee, Wis., Brooklyn, N. Y., Los Angeles, Calif.

Schlitz Beer, 1956

Your thirst can "feel" the difference!

No harsh bitterness! Your taste can actually "feel" the difference between Schlitz and any other beer. A soothing, cooling, refreshing difference you can really feel as well as taste. What a wonderful feeling! No other beer refreshes like Schlitz.

In the Schlitz original HALF-QUART can (packed 24 to the case), also in the convenient 6-pak with the handy handle that makes it so easy to carry.

If you like beer you'll love Schlitz

The Beer that Made Milwaukee Famous

©1955 – Jos. Schlitz Brewing Company, Milwaukee, Wis., Brooklyn, N. Y., Los Angeles, Cal

Schlitz Beer, 1953

"I'm glad they still brew a beer like this!"

BREWED IN THE GREAT TRADITION

Miller
HIGH LIFE

ONLY IN MILWAUKEE

Miller Beer, 1957

BY THE MASTER VINTNERS OF ASTI CELLARS

PRODUCED IN LIMITED QUANTITY

ASTI

ASTI CALIFORNIA Riesling

FINE CALIFORNIA *Wines* FROM THE

VINEYARDS OF WORLD-FAMOUS WINE DISTRICTS

Asti Wine, 1952

▶ *Creme de Menthe, 1957*

Moet Champagne, 1952

Pol Roger Champagne, 1957

Piper-Heidsieck Champagne, 1958 ◄   Mumms Champagne, 1955

Great Western Champagne, 1958   ► Calvert Whiskey, 1950

Wolfschmidt has the secret of Christmas cheer

It's in this brilliantly styled Cocktail Pitcher brimming with wonderful Wolfschmidt Vodka. The secret, of course, is our exclusive refining process that makes Wolfschmidt cleaner, clearer—a happy companion to almost anything liquid. And this gay sparkling Wolfschmidt Cocktail Pitcher carries its usefulness to every season. It comes beautifully gift wrapped at no extra cost. An exciting gift for personal and business friends . . . for their Christmas stockings . . . or stocking for the New Year. Jolly thought: why not a case? Merry Wolfschmidt!

GENERAL WINE & SPIRITS CO., N.Y. 22, N.Y. • MADE FROM GRAIN, 100 OR 80 PROOF. PRODUCT OF U.S.A.

King Blended Whiskey, 1952 ◄   *Wolfschmidt Vodka, 1958*   ▶ *Seagram's Gin, 1957*   ▶ ▶ *Black & White Scotch Whiskey, 1950*

WONDERFULLY...

your gin drinks COME TO LIFE

with Seagram's, "the gin with the golden touch"

REFLECTION ... of PERFECTION
Seagram's 7 Crown

"IT LEAVES YOU BREATHLESS!" says Benny Goodman

Smooth, flawless Smirnoff gives you everything you ask for in a vodka. And nothing you don't want! Having virtually no taste of its own, it never "takes over" in your drinks. It has no "breath"... leaves no whisper of liquor on your lips. Let nobody tell you all vodkas are the same. Make sure you get the one and only Smirnoff. Just mention our name!

the vodka of vodkas

Smirnoff THE GREATEST NAME IN VODKA

80 AND 100 PROOF. DISTILLED FROM GRAIN. STE. PIERRE SMIRNOFF FLS. (DIVISION OF HEUBLEIN). HARTFORD, CONN.

Smirnoff Vodka, 1958

WHAT DOES SMIRNOFF VODKA TASTE LIKE? "Nobody ever tasted Smirnoff," says Wally Cox, "because it doesn't hardly have a taste. It's just sort of willing!" When you mix a jigger of Smirnoff Vodka in orange juice, *it tastes like orange juice;* when you pour Smirnoff in ginger ale, it tastes *like ginger ale!* You don't have to learn new recipes to make delicious drinks with Smirnoff Vodka. Just use Smirnoff instead of gin in your dry martini, collins or tonic—or add a jigger of Smirnoff to any fruit juice or soft drink you like. It's a revelation!

the vodka of vodkas

Smirnoff THE GREATEST NAME IN VODKA

80 AND 100 PROOF. DISTILLED FROM GRAIN. STE. PIERRE SMIRNOFF FLS. (DIVISION OF HEUBLEIN). HARTFORD, CONNECTICUT.

Smirnoff Vodka, 1957

GOLDEN JIGGER and pouring lip impart grace and ease to serving—simply remove jigger, tip, and pour.

Genuine OLD FITZGERALD in the Candlelight Decanter

Bonded Bourbon by Stitzel-Weller... none finer to gladden the throat of man! Decanter by the famous Walter Landor... to add high-fashion flair to an old-fashioned whiskey! Its convenience and decorative after-uses make doubly welcome your gift of OLD FITZGERALD... the final choice of mature tastes.

Candlelight Decanter costs no more than regular fifth.

Your key to Hospitality

KENTUCKY STRAIGHT BOURBON WHISKEY · BONDED 100 PROOF · STITZEL-WELLER DISTILLERY, ESTABLISHED LOUISVILLE, KY., 1849

Seagram's 7 Crown, 1950 ◄   *Old Fitzgerald Bourbon Whiskey, 1955*

same fine Old Forester   in striking new decanter

NO BETTER WAY TO GIVE THE BEST

The finest of fine bonded bourbons, in this exquisite decanter by famed Raymond Loewy. Truly the gift to be given with pride, for there is nothing better in the market. Same price as standard fifth.

Old Forester

KENTUCKY STRAIGHT BOURBON WHISKY · BOTTLED IN BOND · 100 PROOF · BROWN-FORMAN DISTILLERS CORPORATION · AT LOUISVILLE IN KENTUCKY

Old Forester Bourbon, 1955

for more pure pleasure—have a

Camel

No other cigarette tastes so rich, yet smokes so mild!

YOU BET I'D WALK A MILE FOR A CAMEL!

IT'S A PSYCHOLOGICAL FACT: **PLEASURE HELPS YOUR DISPOSITION**

How's your disposition today?

EVER YIP LIKE A TERRIER when the store sends you the wrong package? That's only natural when little annoyances like this occur. But — it's a psychological fact that pleasure helps your disposition! That's why everyday pleasures — like smoking, for instance — mean so much. So if you're a smoker, it's important to smoke the *most pleasure-giving cigarette* — Camel.

R. J. Reynolds Tobacco Co., Winston-Salem, N. C.

For more pure pleasure—have a Camel

"I've tried 'em all — but it's Camels for me!" *Rock Hudson*

YOU CAN SEE RUGGED ROCK HUDSON STARRING IN U-I'S "NEVER SAY GOODBYE"

CAMEL TURKISH & DOMESTIC BLEND CIGARETTES — CHOICE QUALITY

No other cigarette is so rich-tasting yet so mild !

ROCK HUDSON AGREES with Camel smokers everywhere: there *is* more pure pleasure in Camels! More flavor, genuine mildness! Good reasons why today more people smoke Camels than any other cigarette

Remember this: pleasure helps your disposition. And for *more* pure pleasure — have a Camel!

Camel Cigarettes, 1956 ◄ *Camel Cigarettes, 1956*

How MILD can a Cigarette be?

MAKE THE 30-DAY CAMEL MILDNESS TEST—SEE WHY...

MORE PEOPLE SMOKE CAMELS
than any other cigarette!

MAN'S IDEA OF A MOVIE HERO
And the women agree! 6 feet 4 inches, John Wayne has smashed his way to fame in dozens of knock-down-and-drag-out — hard-riding ... glorious motion pictures!

"The roles I play in movies are far from easy on my voice — I can't risk throat irritation. So I smoke Camels — they're mild"

John Wayne

POPULAR, HANDSOME HOLLYWOOD STAR

"I've been around movie sets long enough to know how important cigarette mildness is to an actor. So when it came to deciding what cigarette was just right for my throat — I was very particular. I made a *sensible* test—my own 30-Day Camel Mildness Test!

"I gave Camels a real tryout for 30 days. The most pleasure I ever had from smoking. My own 'T-Zone' told me just how mild and good tasting a cigarette can be! I found out for myself why *more people smoke Camels than any other cigarette!*"

R. J. Reynolds Tobacco Company, Winston-Salem, N. C.

Make your own 30-Day Camel MILDNESS Test in your "T-Zone"

(T for Throat, T for Taste)

Not one single case of throat irritation *due to smoking*
CAMELS!

Yes, these were the findings of noted throat specialists after a total of 2,470 weekly examinations of the throats of hundreds of men and women who smoked Camels — and only Camels — for 30 consecutive days.

Camel Cigarettes, 1951

PALL MALL

FAMOUS CIGARETTES

·IN HOC SIGNO VINCES·

"WHEREVER PARTICULAR
PEOPLE CONGREGATE"

YOU
CAN LIGHT
EITHER
END!

Atomic/
Defense
42

READY AS
A RIFLE BULLET

America has an arsenal
of operational missiles.
Their 'readiness' is a tribute
to the ability of private
industry to lend full support to
government and military effort.
A high percentage of the
rocket power plants for these
missiles was developed and
produced by Aerojet-General,
a subsidiary of The General
Tire and Rubber Company.

AEROJET-GENERAL

CORPORATION,

AZUSA AND SACRAMENTO,

CALIFORNIA

General Tire

pioneer

in

FIRE

Wanted...
More Men Like Mike !

—men who want to go places, and have plenty of the stuff it takes to get there!

Mike lived a lively American boyhood. An average student, a popular athlete, he finished high school in '46, decided to start building a career in the Army.

Mike could be any one of a thousand typical young career men who are going places in today's Army. He could be you!

Careful studies of Mike's personal aptitudes led to his selection for technical training in tanks and other armored vehicles. He took to it like a duck to water!

Finishing technical school as a Private, First Class, Mike progressed steadily in skill, efficiency and rank. Each year he took a 30-day vacation trip, with pay.

Mike studied, worked, watched his chances. Finished his first "hitch" as a Sergeant. During leave he went home and married his high school sweetheart.

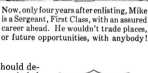

Now, only four years after enlisting, Mike is a Sergeant, First Class, with an assured career ahead. He wouldn't trade places, or future opportunities, with anybody!

The young man of today who wants to get ahead can continue his education and start building a career at the same time, in the new U. S. Army. More than 200 courses of specialized training for many different career fields are taught in the various Army schools. Each man's abilities are charted, to place him where he should develop rapidly. Working with career-minded young men like himself on the frontiers of military science, he can serve his country with true professional pride. Today's U.S. Army is providing excellent career opportunities for America's finest young men.

U. S. ARMY

VISIT YOUR NEAREST U. S. ARMY AND U. S. AIR FORCE RECRUITING STATION

INVISIBLE JET FIGHTER MAKES TEST FLIGHT

This Grumman jet fighter is invisible. She is electrons. Yet day after day, she makes supersonic flights through an electronic sky.

Actually she is an electronic brain by name of REAC (Reeves Electronic Analog Computer) directed by a group of brilliant human brains. The latter convert the mathematics of the aircraft into a language they and she understand. They "tell" her everything they know about the new fighter design through wired panels and curves wired on revolving drums.

The cockpit with its human pilot is plugged in. At a signal he takes off and climbs to fifty thousand feet. The electronic air is smooth up to the transonic range where sound waves pile up until the air misbehaves. Once through, the air is smooth again, and they are ready to test a combat maneuver at supersonic speed.

"Now decelerate."

The pilot extends speed brakes. All eyes watch the instruments, and the reactions recorded on moving graph paper.

These performance data, gained months before actual flight tests, help check designs created with results from other Grumman research. One reason Grumman planes are ready in quantity when needed.

GRUMMAN AIRCRAFT ENGINEERING CORPORATION · BETHPAGE · LONG ISLAND · NEW YORK

Designers and builders of the Cougar jet fighter, the S2F-1 sub-killer, the Albatross amphibian, metal boats, and Aerobilt truck bodies.

Grumman Aircraft Engineering Corporation, 1954

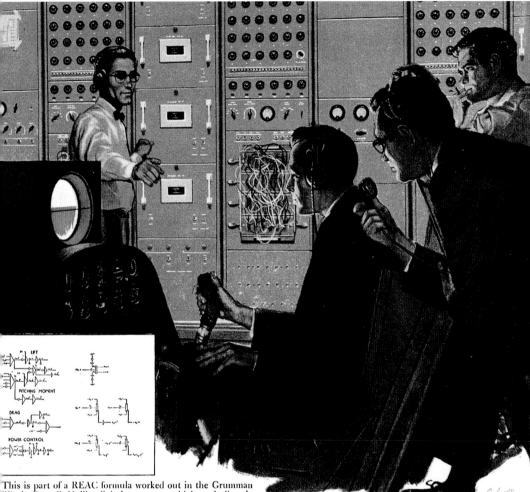

This is part of a REAC formula worked out in the Grumman "Brain Room". Unlike digital computers which work directly with numbers, this analog computer works with forces of motion by reproducing them in volts.

The computer is "told" the facts of the problem through miniature switchboards. A different problem can be made known to the computer quickly, simply by changing boards.

Some data, like wind tunnel results, are fed into the computer from revolving drums. The computer gets its information electrically from copper wires glued over penciled curves.

These are typical REAC answers. Engineers translate these squiggles into design information. Sometimes thousands of such answers may be required to solve any one of the many design problems.

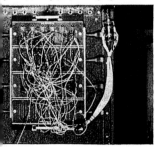

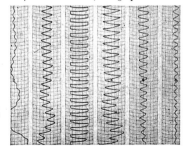

You'd fly like this

without the vital accessories created by AiResearch to make possible today's high-speed, high-altitude flight

NEW "LUNGS" FOR THE LUXURY AIRLINERS!

When you're flying at 20,000 feet and you sit there warm and comfortable, breathing clean fresh air, you reap the benefit of years of painstaking development work by AiResearch engineers.

"Living room" comfort in the newest high-altitude airliners like the Super Constellation, the Martin 404 and the Convair 340 is the work of AiResearch.

The air you breathe is scooped up from the outside, compressed and refrigerated or heated —

delivered inside the cabin at just the right temperature.

On supersonic jets and turbo-props even greater problems of air conditioning are conquered by AiResearch equipment.

Every American-built, high-speed, high-altitude airplane flies with the aid of products manufactured by AiResearch.

Would you like to work with us? Qualified engineers, scientists and skilled craftsmen are needed now at AiResearch.

In a modern airliner at 20,000 feet or higher, you are not only comfortable, but you fly *safer* and *faster*. Vital "lung" in the pressurizing system is the AiResearch cabin supercharger. Together with the AiResearch refrigeration unit, it keeps the plane air conditioned in the air or on the ground.

AiResearch Manufacturing Company

A DIVISION OF THE GARRETT CORPORATION

LOS ANGELES 45, CALIFORNIA • PHOENIX, ARIZONA

DESIGNER AND MANUFACTURER OF AIRCRAFT EQUIPMENT IN THESE MAJOR CATEGORIES

Air Turbine Refrigeration   Heat Transfer Equipment   Electric Actuators   Gas Turbines   Cabin Superchargers   Pneumatic Power Units   Electronic Controls   Cabin Pressure Controls   Temperature Controls

AiResearch Manufacturing Company, 1952   ▶ *Republic Aviation, 1954*   ▶ ▶ *Sperry Gyroscope Company, 1954*   ▶ ▶ ▶ *Aerojet General Corporation, 195*

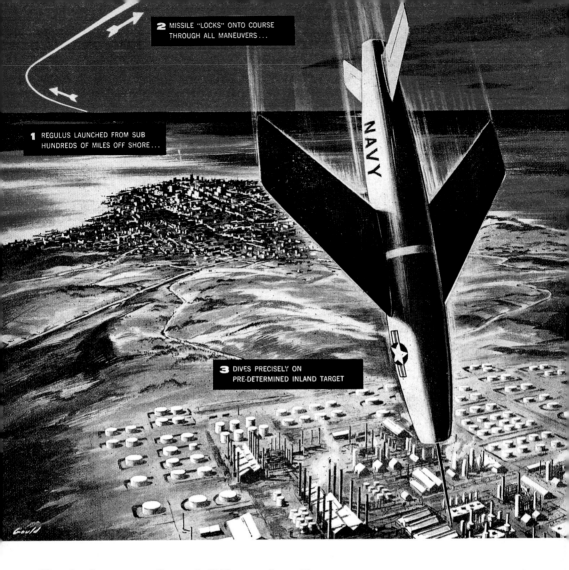

2 MISSILE "LOCKS" ONTO COURSE THROUGH ALL MANEUVERS...

1 REGULUS LAUNCHED FROM SUB HUNDREDS OF MILES OFF SHORE...

3 DIVES PRECISELY ON PRE-DETERMINED INLAND TARGET

Sub-Launched Missile Gives Navy New Striking Power

CONTROL OF REGULUS HELD "UNCANNY"..."BIRDS" CAN BE RETRIEVED DURING TESTS

THE STORY BEHIND THE STORY:

■ When a guided missile launched from a submarine hundreds of miles off shore can be held to an accurate course at speeds approaching Mach 1, and precisely aimed at a specific inland target— that's news, *bad* news for a possible enemy. And, when costly models of the missile can be recovered and re-used time after time for evaluation and training, that's news, too — *good* news for American taxpayers.

■ On both counts, the Navy's Regulus, developed by Chance Vought Aircraft, Inc., is constantly in the headlines.

■ Providing the stability that holds Regulus on its course with a vise-like grip —and assuring recovery during tests—is a specially-designed Automatic Pilot, created by Sperry. Like its relative, the famous Sperry Gyropilot* Flight Control favored by the military and leading airlines, this electronic "brain" is sensitive to the slightest signal change in the flight path. Under its command, powerful servos or "muscles" of the control system

make instant corrections — fly Regul unfailingly through intricate maneuve at all speeds and at all altitudes.

■ There's a mighty difference betwee the automatic controls created by Sper for this newest guided missile of t Navy, and those provided by Sperry f the Navy's first guided missile back World War I days. But they're alike this respect: Both resulted from unmatched combination of skillful en neering *plus* specialized experience electronics and gyroscopics, and precisi in production. *T M REG. U.S. PAT.*

ON SHORT RUNWAYS, AIR FORCE PILOTS CAN SAVE THEIR BRAKES AND TIRES BY RELEASING SPECIAL LANDING PARACHUTE FROM THE TAIL OF THE B-47.

POWERED AND PROTECTED BY G.

THE B-47 IS OUR FASTEST BOMBER

Six G-E Jet Engines Power Boeing Bomber: G-E Armament System Protects It

The Air Force's B-47, fastest known bomber in the world, is a sleek, swept-wing aircraft, powered by six mighty G-E jet engines. A medium bomber of 600 mph class, it can fly 3000 miles, at an altitude of over seven miles. For protection against enemy attack, it is being equipped with a General Electric radar-controlled gunfire system which can operate even at night or in poor visibility. The complex plane is manned by three highly trained Air Force officers—pilot, co-pilot, and navigator-bombardier.

The Air Force called upon General Electric to supply the power and armament systems for the B-47 because military men recognized G.E.'s long history of engineering leadership. For instance, General Electric has supplied armament systems for several other types of military aircraft before the Boeing B-47, turbo-superchargers for piston-engine planes since 1921, and jet engines since 1942. And, of course, the Air Force knew that General Electric would have the production help of thou-

sands of "small-business" subcontracto suppliers. Our nation's defense is our m portant problem, and it takes all kinds o nesses, large and small, all working toge assure our continued freedom. General I Company, Schenectady 5, N. Y.

ENGINEERS: General Electric is constantly adding t of highly skilled engineers and scientists. If you have ground of successful, creative engineering, and are n defense production, send your qualifications to our Personnel Service Dept., Section B, Schenectady 5, N

*You can put your confidence in_*

GENERAL ⓖⓔ ELECTRIC

1903—Wright Brothers make first powered flight at Kitty Hawk

1910—Eugene Ely takes off from deck of converted battleship

1918—American pilots engage in daring aerial combat over France

1919—Navy flying boat makes first successful trans-Atlantic flight

1921—G-E supercharged Air Corps plane sets altitude record

1942—G-E powered Bell P-59, first US jet, test-flown at Muroc, Calif.

1944—Boeing B-29 uses first G-E electronic gunfire system

1953—G-E powered North American F-86 outscores MIG

50TH ANNIVERSARY OF POWERED FLIGHT — PROGRESS · SECURITY

G-E ENGINEERS rely upon their experience, ingenuity, and mechanical aids such as the digital computer to accomplish such engineering triumphs as jet engines and radar fire-control systems.

PRODUCTION of complex equipment depends upon advanced engineering techniques and skilled use of modern, costly machinery. Often, a new machine must be designed for one specific job.

General Electric, 1953 ◄◄   Hitco, 1952 ◄   Midvac Steels, 1952   ► Caterpillar, 1958   ►► Lukens Steel Company, 1951

This one was only a test (atomic detonation in Nevada).

Big reason for better roads

"It has been determined as a matter of Federal policy," reports the President's Advisory Committee on a National Highway Program, "that at least 70 million people would have to be evacuated from target areas in case of threatened or actual enemy attack. No urban area in the country today has highway facilities equal to this task."

But such highways are coming: the 41,000-mile National System of Interstate and Defense Highways.

This tremendous network of no-stop freeways offers other vital defense benefits, too. Obviously, it will speed the movement of men and materiel. But more importantly, it will encourage the decentralization of our industries. Already more and more plants are following these fine new roads out of congested cities, out into the wide countryside just minutes away by swift, safe freeways.

WHAT EVERY CITIZEN SHOULD KNOW

Don't allow the Interstate-Defense Highway Program to bog down. Find out how it will serve you, how much it will actually cost, how long it will take to finish. Send today for a free copy of an informative booklet, "The Road Ahead." Write Dept. 12T, Caterpillar Tractor Co., Peoria, Illinois, U.S.A.

CATERPILLAR
REG. U. S. PAT. OFF.

Diesel Engines • Tractors • Motor Graders • Earthmoving Equipment

THE WORLD'S NO. 1 ROAD BUILDING EQUIPMENT

Atomic Energy...

...or Medicine

*Fabricated by
an equipment builder
using the Lukenomics principle.*

Here's a sample of Lukenomics coordination at work. For high purity in Chloromycetin—vital new antibiotic—acid adjustment tanks and fermentation units were built of Lukens Inconel-Clad Steel with specially polished interiors. *Bonus* results: low initial cost, minimum maintenance, special resistance to corrosion threats of salt and other chemicals. And—by use of *clad*—the builder also saved critical amounts of one of today's scarce metals.

... whatever your business, if it depends on a production or process operation, consider this: *in the current emergency, how long can you keep on producing?* Here's an idea that may help.

There are progressive *equipment builders* who specialize today in delivering new production potentials despite current shortages. Coordination of the major factors in equipment design, including problem exploration, is the key.

This coordination of effort we call Lukenomics. Through it, such equipment builders combine their specialized experience, and that of competent designers and engineers, with Lukens' knowledge of materials, their production and use.

We can put you in touch with such builders. Write today, outlining your problem. Manager, Marketing Service, Lukens Steel Company, 476 Lukens Building, Coatesville, Pa.

Promote steel production generally—speed sale of your scrap.

LUKENS

LUKENS STEEL COMPANY

OVER 140 YEARS EXPERIENCE AS THE WORLD'S LEADING PRODUCER OF SPECIALTY STEEL PRODUCTS

STEEL PLATE   CLAD STEELS   HEADS   STEEL PLATE SHAPES

Even this cloud

as a silver lining

Margin for Error . . . *None!*

You swing into your final approach. At precisely the right instant the Landing Signal Officer flags you to cut your power—and you're aboard! ☆ Such skill and precision is indicative of that which is required today in *every* phase of the aircraft industry. The bearings in modern jet turbines, for instance, must be held to accurate tolerances measured in millionths of an inch. That's why the leading jet turbine manufacturers specify Bower aircraft bearings first. Their exceptional high quality and unerring precision allow Bower bearings to stand unbelievable turbine speeds and temperatures—that match the supersonic speeds of today's jet aircraft—*with a minimum of lubrication.* ☆ Whatever *you* produce, if it uses bearings, specify Bower! Choose from a complete line of tapered, straight and journal roller bearings for every field of transportation and industry.

BOWER ROLLER BEARING DIVISION
FEDERAL-MOGUL-BOWER BEARINGS, INC., DETROIT 14, MICH.

○ BOWER

ROLLER BEARINGS

IDEALLY SUITED TO HIGH-SPEED OPERATION

Built to hold their precision indefinitely, these aircraft bearings are recommended wherever superior quality and high-speed operation are required. For some applications, a special alloy steel—developed jointly by Bower and several aircraft companies—is used.

FLYING SAUCERS...REAL!

One type of instrument a weather balloon carries aloft is the radiosonde. What this inexpensive little weather observer can do is just short of magic ... for it reports continuously—by radio—the temperature, pressure, and humidity of the upper air.

Key parts of radiosonde are temperature and humidity elements and a disc-shaped, pressure-responsive diaphragm that supplies the all-important pressure "reference".

United States Gauge has a special gift for making aneroid diaphragms or cells—a distinction acquired over many years, and narrowed to ± two-millibar accuracy by uncompromising requirements for similar cells in complex parachute control and navigation instruments.

U. S. Gauge makes radiosonde diaphragms from Ni-Span C—an alloy with a constant thermal modulus—to cancel temperature effects. Compensating thermal influence of the instrument components within the diaphragm design was another—and tough—problem. USG licked it—hopes to tackle one for you.

If you require diaphragms like those we've described ... if you have any product in need of accurate temperature or pressure-sensing elements or instruments, let USG creative instrumentation go to work for you. United States Gauge, Division of American Machine and Metals, Inc., Sellersville, Pa.

PRODUCTS OF UNITED STATES GAUGE ... Absolute Pressure Gauges
Aircraft Instruments • Air Volume Controls • Altitude Gauges • Boiler Gauges
Chemical Gauges • Mercury Gas and Vapor Dial Thermometers • Glass Tube
and Industrial Thermometers • Flow Meters • Inspectors' Test Gauges
Precision Laboratory Test Gauges • Marine, Ship and Air-Brake Gauges
Voltmeters • Ammeters • Welding Gauges

OTHER DIVISIONS OF AMERICAN MACHINE AND METALS, INC. AT SELLERSVILLE, PA.: GOTHAM INSTRUMENTS, AND AUTOBAR SYSTEMS

Creative Instrumentation   UNITED STATES GAUGE

GARCIA

USG

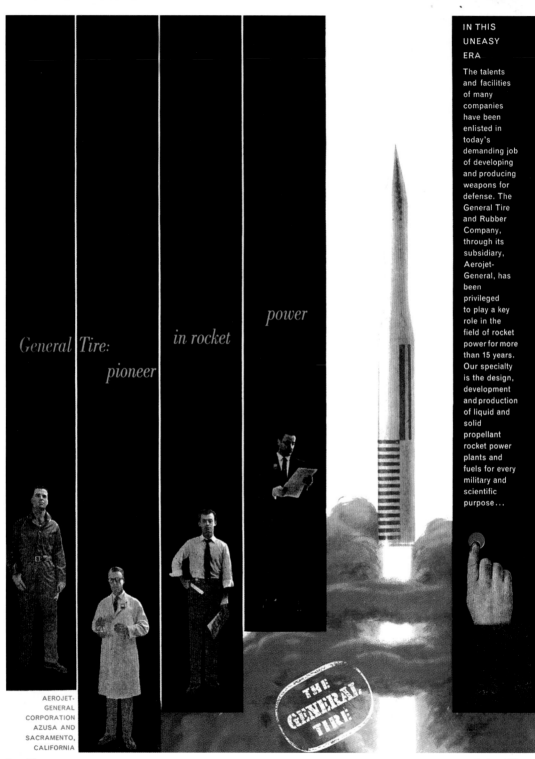

General Tire: pioneer in rocket power

AEROJET-GENERAL CORPORATION AZUSA AND SACRAMENTO, CALIFORNIA

THE GENERAL TIRE

General Tire, 1955

▶ General Tire, 1958

eneral Tire:

ioneer in

ocket power

ESTINATION: *known*

rth-shaking...ear-shattering...
-searing, these are words that
rtially describe the terrifying
e-off of today's

cket powered missiles.

rojet-General is a pioneer in this
l new field and the nation's leading
ducer of both liquid and solid

pellant rocket power plants.

rojet-General is a subsidiary of
General Tire and Rubber Company.

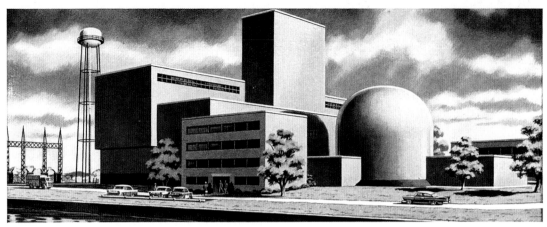

Enrico Fermi atomic power plant *is under way near Detroit through the joint efforts of 18 electric companies. A group of equipment manufacturers and the Atomic Energy Commission are also associated in the project.*

Dresden, Illinois, plant *is being developed by 7 electric light and power companies, their equipment manufacturers, and with the co-operation of the AEC.*

Yankee atomic-electric plant *is being developed by 12 New England electric companies. A number of equipment manufacturers and the AEC are participating.*

What will atomic-electric power plants look like?

Among the atomic-electric power plants now under way, three will look like the drawings above when completed.

Although they appear somewhat alike, each involves different methods, different materials, a different type of atomic reactor or "furnace." That's because the electric companies, the equipment manufacturers and the U. S. Atomic Energy Commission—who are all participating in atomic development—are searching for the best ways to produce electricity, using atomic energy as fuel.

The development of atomic-powered electric plants is the latest stage in bringing plentiful electricity to America. You can be sure that electric company skills and experience, acquired in 75 years of service, are being applied to this great new job.

America's Independent Electric Light and Power Companies*

Company names on request through this magazine

Atomic Electric Power, 1957

▶ American Bosch Arma Corporation, 195⬛

Now you can protect precious lives with

An all-concrete blast-resistant house

Here's a house with all the advantages of any concrete house—PLUS protection from atomic blasts at minimum cost.

A firesafe, attractive, *low-annual-cost* house, it provides comfortable living—PLUS a refuge for your family in this atomic age.

The blast-resistant house design is based on principles learned at Hiroshima and Nagasaki and at Eniwetok and Yucca Flats. It has a reinforced concrete first floor and roof and reinforced concrete masonry walls. The walls, the floor and the roof are tied together securely with reinforcement to form a rigidly integrated house that the engineers calculate will resist blast pressures 40% closer to bursts than conventionally-built houses.

Anywhere in the concrete basement of the house would be much safer than above ground but a special shelter area has been provided in this basement to protect occupants from blast pressures expected at distances as close as 3,600 feet from ground zero of a bomb with an explosive force equivalent to 20,000 tons of TNT. This shelter area affords protection from radiation, fire and flying debris as well. And the same shelter area also can serve as a refuge from the lesser violence of tornadoes, hurricanes and earthquakes.

The safety features built into this blast-resistant house are estimated by the architect and engineer to raise the cost less than 10%.

Concrete always has been known for its remarkable strength and durability. That's why it can be used economically to build houses with a high degree of safety from atomic blasts.

Like all concrete structures, blast-resistant concrete houses are moderate in first cost, require little maintenance and give long years of service. The result is *low-annual-cost* shelter. Write for folder.

PORTLAND CEMENT ASSOCIATION
Dept. A6-9, 33 West Grand Avenue, Chicago 10, Illinois
A national organization to improve and extend the uses of portland cement and concrete through scientific research and engineering field work.

Interiors of a blast-resistant house have all the charm and livability of conventional houses.

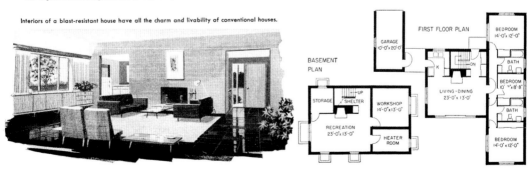

Portland Cement Association, 1955

Auto— mobiles '70

The most beautiful thing on wheels

DOLLAR FOR DOLLAR

you can't beat a

PONTIAC

NOTHING NEAR PONTIAC'S MODEST PRICE

OFFERS ITS *SUPERLATIVE* BEAUTY, PERFORMANCE AND LONG RANGE ECONOM

Dollar for Dollar you can't beat a
Pontiac

All it needs is <u>you</u> behind the wheel!

It's only human to get a glow when others view your car with admiring eyes. The satisfaction of Plymouth owners doesn't end here. For they know that their car contains admirable traits you can't see in a glance— advanced engineering, quality materials, honest craftsmanship, and an enduring performance that constantly sustains their judgment in choosing a Plymouth.

PLYMOUTH

Chrysler Corporation's No. 1 C

The Plymouth Cranbrook Convertible Club Coupe, shown at the Shadow Mountain Club, Palm Desert, near Palm Springs, Cali

New Yorker DeLuxe 4-door Sedan

Now on display

AMERICA'S **FIRST FAMILY** OF FINE CARS

New Yorker DeLuxe Convertible— *New Yorker and New Yorker DeLuxe in 9 body styles*

A stunning new mood in **Highway Fashion!**

Never before has such a brilliant array of fine motor cars been introduced to the American public . . . styled to create a glamorous new mood in Highway Fashion . . . and embodying the kind of engineering the world associates with Chrysler performance and safety!

And here is a *range* of cars unequalled anywhere. The beautiful Windsor line . . . lowest-priced of all Chryslers. The spectacular New Yorker . . . whose performance has all America talking. The matchless Imperial . . . custom-built for those who demand the absolute finest. All in a variety of body models, colors, and interior trim combinations to suit every need and every wish.

. . . and now on display at your nearby Chrysler dealer's!

The beautiful 1953 **CHRYSLER**

Custom Imperial 4-door Sedan— *Imperial line also includes the Town Limousine*

Windsor Club Coupe— *Windsor and Windsor DeLuxe in 7 body styles*

ontiac, 1950 ◄◄◄   Pontiac, 1951 ◄◄   Plymouth, 1953 ◄   Chrysler, 1952

► Chevrolet, 1953

Here's what's NEW *in motor cars for 1951...*
all in America's Largest and Finest Low-priced Car

plus Chevrolet's time-proved POWER*glide* automatic transmission*

Look—and see! All these *new* things, all these *pleasing* things, all these *proved* things you and your family want in an automobile, are yours in the '51 Chevrolet—*America's largest and finest low-priced car!* You'll find it's outstanding—in size, in styling, in comfort, in Valve-in-Head engine performance, and in time-proved *no-shift* driving or *standard* driving—all at lowest cost. See it, drive it, and you'll *know* it's the smartest buy of the year! Chevrolet Motor Division, *General Motors Corporation*, Detroit 2, Michigan.

Combination of Powerglide automatic transmission and 105-h.p. engine optional on De Luxe models at extra cost.

The *Smart New* Styleline De Luxe 4-Door Sedan

NEW *America-Preferred Bodies by Fisher*

With new and even more strikingly beautiful lines, contours and colors ... with extra-sturdy Fisher Unisteel construction ... Curved Windshield and Panoramic Visibility ... the smartest, safest, most comfortable edition of Chevrolet's America-Preferred Bodies by Fisher.

NEW *Modern-Mode Interiors*

With upholstery and appointments of outstanding quality, in beautiful two-tone color harmonies ... with an even more attractive steering wheel embodying a new full-circle horn ring (in De Luxe models) ... and with extra-generous head, leg and elbow room for driver and all passengers.

NEW *Improved Center-Point Steering*

(and Center-Point Design) Making steering even ea at low speeds or while parking ... just as Chevro famous Unitized Knee-Action Gliding Ride is e fortable beyond comparison in its price range additional reasons why more people buy Chevr any other car.

EW *American Beauty Design*

...nt new styling . . . featuring entirely new ... parking lights, fender moldings and rear-end ... imparting that longer, lower, wider big-... ok which sets Chevrolet above and apart from ...er motor cars in its field.

NEW *More Powerful Jumbo-Drum Brakes*

(with Dubl-Life rivetless brake linings) Largest brakes in the entire low-price field . . . with both brake shoes on each wheel self-energizing for forward and reverse operation of car . . . providing maximum stopping-power with up to 25% less driver effort.

 Safety-Sight Instrument Panel

Safer, more convenient, more efficient . . . having an overhanging upper crown to eliminate reflections in windshield from instrument lights . . . and with plain easy-to-read instruments in two large clusters directly in front of the driver.

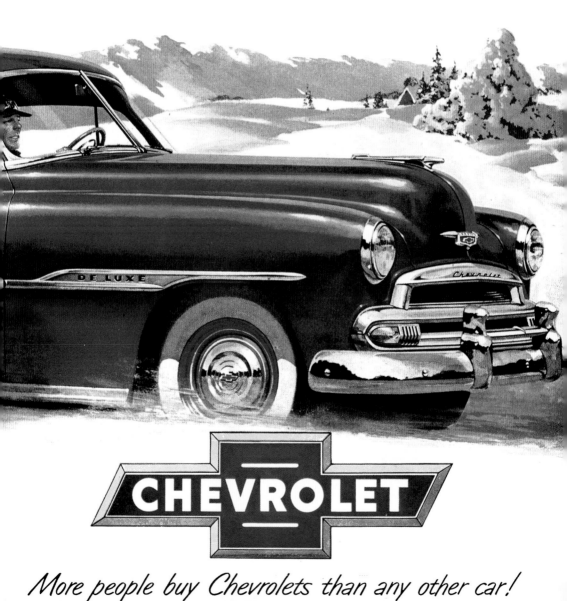

DE LUXE

Chevrolet

CHEVROLET

More people buy Chevrolets than any other car!

Goes a long, long way on a gallon

WILLYS *makes sens*

-IN DESIGN   -IN ECONOMY   -IN USEFULNES

*"We needn't stop for gas
. . . I filled it last week"*

WILLYS *makes sense*

— *IN ECONOMY* — *IN EASE OF DRIVING* — *IN COMFORT*

Star of the silky way

Willys, 1951 ◄◄   Willys, 1951 ◄   Buick Roadmaster, 1953

...e had to be good. It's our ...n Anniversary ROADMASTER.

...t we lavished our skills, our ...nd our time to make it the ...a fifty-year line of fine cars.

...drive it, you will come to know ...a fifty-year best really is.

...ow it in the swift and soaring ...sponse of its V8 Engine. The ...all V8. The first such V8 with ...compression, with vertical ...th 12-volt electrical system, ...ost of modern engineering

You'll know it in the silken velocity of its getaway — with Twin-Turbine Dynaflow adding far swifter, quieter acceleration to infinite smoothness.

You'll know it, too, in the velvety luxury of its bettered ride, in the new ease of its handling, in the more precise control it gives you, in the more reassuring comfort you feel.

For Buick engineers pulled all the stops on this 1953 ROADMASTER. They widened the front tread — compacted the frame—shortened the turn radius— recalibrated the four coil springs— increased the braking power — made

Power Steering standard equipment, and even added Power Brakes* to lighten the task of quick, sure stopping.

But why say more?

It is for you, the beneficiary of all this engineering excellence, to discover the great and gorgeous going of the swiftest, the smoothest, the silkiest, the most silent automobile yet built in half a century of Buick building.

Your Buick dealer will be happy to introduce you two. Why not visit him soon?

BUICK *Division of* GENERAL MOTORS

Optional at extra cost.

...tom *Built* ROADMASTER *by Buick*

WHY BE TIED DOWN ʼ

No longer need you be tied down to the fussiness of yesteryear, to the hea
motion and the glittering pomp. Now you can make your driving as efficie
living. Now you can let a magnificent new Lincoln for 1953 put you in step
effortless power and pace of this century.

For now with Lincoln, everything you touch turns to astonishing power. ʼ
the wheel, and two tons of flawless engineering turn with incredible ease—
the unique combination of power steering and exclusive ball-joint front v
pension. You touch the brake, and again two tons do your bidding, as powe
braking. You even touch buttons on your seat, and power moves you not on!
or backward, but also up or down as you wish. The seat even adjusts to you

Standard equipment, accessories, and trim illustrated are subject to change without notice.
Power steering, power elevator seats, power brakes, white side-wall tires optional at extra cost.

LINCOLN

THE ONE FINE CAR DESIGNED FOR MODERN LIVING
—POWERED TO LEAVE THE PAST FAR BEHIND

Crowning achievement of Ford Motor Company's 50th
Anniversary—"50 Years Forward on the American Road"

ESTERDAY ?

then--then you touch the accelerator and the new V-205 engine is at your
nd. That's V-205 for 205 horsepower in the new V-8 power plant that brought
n first, second, third *and* fourth places in the stock car division of the Mexican
merican Race, called the toughest automobile competition in the world.
all of this power is contained in the shape of things to come--the Lincoln
that breaks sharply with the past. Clean lined, without gingerbread or super-
brightwork, it is a superb achievement in functional design, dramatized by the
azzling colors and fabrics that ever took to the road. Come accept Lincoln's in-
n to depart from the past. Your Lincoln dealer awaits you with a Lincoln Cos-
tan or Capri.
LINCOLN DIVISION — FORD MOTOR COMPANY

There are few occasions in a motorist's life that are so surprising or delightful as his first ride behind the wheel of a new Cadillac. For, in that single journey, he discovers power and responsiveness—and handling ease and comfort—he never imagined possible in a motor car. It is, in essence, an education in all the good things of motordom. If you are still looking forward to this extraordinary experience, we urge you to visit your Cadillac dealer soon. The car is waiting for you now—waiting to give you the most revealing ride of your life!

Jewels by

Cadillac

CADILLAC MOTOR CAR DIVISION ★ GENERAL MOTORS CORPORATION

Cadillac

by Harry Winston

It Will Add to Your Happiness!

There is a great *plus* value that comes with a Cadillac which is very difficult for anyone to evaluate—except a Cadillac owner. To put it briefly, a Cadillac adds a goodly measure of happiness to a family's daily existence. It is not just the satisfaction which comes from fine performance and extraordinary comfort and out-

standing safety and handling ease—thrilling though these things can be. It is more a sense of pride and family well-being—a joy of possession—and a consciousness of membership in the world's most distinguished group of motor car owners. Although difficult to explain and define—Cadillac owners from all sections

of the country can testify that it is very real and very valuable—a most moving reason for moving up to Cadillac. And remember—all this is in *addition* to the innumerable *practical* reasons for owning a Cadillac. It's too much to miss—any longer. Better see your Cadillac dealer right away. He'll be delighted to see you.

It rolls out the red carpet wherever you g

YOU find an exultant satisfaction at the wheel of a 1954 ROADMASTER that you find in precious few other motorcars.

When you take that wheel — or relinquish it to an attendant — you do so with a special pride.

For this great Buick is an impressive automobile — in size and length and breadth and beauty.

It has, as you can see, a serene look of luxury and the unmistakable mark of true style modernity. Both are recognized immediately by all who see it.

Then, of course, there is the royal treatment you enjoy *underway* in ROADMASTER.

It's in the easy cruising sweep of its great 200-horsepower V8 engine — and in the incredibly smooth delivery of this power through Twin-Turbine Dynaflow.

It's in the wondrous visibility provided by the back-swept windshield — and the advanced comfort of high-air ventilation.

It's in the masterful levelness of ride that comes from a blending of engineering features found in no other car in the world.

MILTON BERLE STARS FOR BUICK
See the
Buick-Berle Show
Tuesday evenings

And it's in the literally luxuri handling you find at your fin tips with Buick Safety Po Steering. It's in the added conv ience, optional at extra cost Power Brakes, power-positio front seat, power-operated ra antenna.

You need but one look at, one in, one arrival with ROADMAS to know what tremendous satis tion is to be had here.

Your Buick dealer will gladly range matters. See him soon.

BUICK *Division of* GENERAL MOT

When better automobiles are bu BUICK will build them

ROADMASTER *Custom Built by* BUICK

Hand-buffed leather in coral and ivory, deep-pile matching carpet and colour-keyed instrument panel and wheel typify the luxurious new interiors of the '54 Custom Catalinas.

Dollar for Dollar You Can't Beat a

PONTIAC

A GENERAL MOTORS MASTERPIECE

America's First Low Cost Luxury Car

You are looking at the new wonder of the motoring world, the completely new Star Chief Pontiac. And what makes this car such a wonder is its unsurpassed combination of superb quality and low price. *There has never been anything like it.* For here is the biggest, richest and most powerful Pontiac ever built—qualified by length, luxury, styling and per-

formance to rank with the very finest cars. Yet the proud and beautiful Star Chief can adorn your driveway no matter how carefully you budget your car expenditures. It is still comfortably within the price range just above the lowest!

And America's first low cost luxury car is only half the great news from Pontiac. For 1954, the Chieftain, General Motors

lowest priced eight, is also mightier than ever and far more beautiful inside and out—again the dominant dollar for dollar value at its very modest cost. Check Pontiac's remarkable secret for '54. See, drive and price these distinguished new Silver Streak Pontiacs. Prove to your pleasure and profit that never before have quality and low cost been so beautifully combined.

DON'T MISS DAVE GARROWAY'S NIGHTTIME SHOW—NBC-TV • PONTIAC MOTOR DIVISION OF GENERAL MOTORS CORPORATION

Pontiac, 1954

You compress time....distance - in effortless ease with the first complete driver control

You cannot pass unnoticed in a stunning car like this. Exuberant new color and bold sweep of line draw the eye like a magnet. But flattering and thrilling, too, is your new power over time and distance. PowerFlite, most automatic of all no-clutch transmissions, multiplies your safety with control of motion that's entirely new. The 235 HP FirePower V-8 engine gives you instant power for instant response at all times. Power Steering is easy and safe as pointing. Power Brakes halt you swiftly and surely with but ⅓ the pedal pressure of conventional brakes. All these combine in the first complete driver control. A new day in driving ease and safety. A new day that is yours to enjoy just as soon as you visit your nearby Chrysler dealer.

2nd look

The Power of Leadership is yours in a **BEAUTIFUL CHRYSLER**

Chrysler, 1954

More than the grace of greatness

HERE stands, in literal fact, the finest automobile that the great Buick factories have ever been privileged to build.

It is the biggest of Buicks, the best of Buicks, and in our book, that puts it well up toward the head of the class in the fine-car field.

You see outward evidence of what we mean in the fresh modernity of its styling, and its brand-new bodies to bring this about.

There is, as you can see, a spectacular expanse of greater glass area, and back-sweeping windshield that bring a new visibility to driving.

There are new and more spacious

interiors, a new high-air ventilation system, a new instrument panel with a completely new speedometer which you read at the horizontal.

But there's more to the greatness of the ROADMASTER than meets the eye.

Its V8 engine attains a new high of 200 horsepower, linked, incidentally, with the new economy of Power-Head Pistons.

Its power delivery is suaved to pure silkiness by the new and even quieter Twin-Turbine Dynaflow.

Its wheelbase is longer, its center of gravity is lower, its front-end

suspension is newly designed to an even finer control on curves, and its ride is more perfectly leveled and poised.

Safety Power Steering is yours at no additional charge, and you have, at your extra-cost option, the added convenience of Power Brakes, Air Conditioning, a four-way power-positioned front seat, and power-operated radio aerial.

So we invite you to see this newest and finest of fine cars for 1954. A visit to your Buick dealer will be, we believe, a revealing and rewarding experience.

BUICK Division of GENERAL MOTORS When better automobiles are built Buick will build them

MILTON BERLE STARS FOR BUICK—See the Buick-Berle Show Tuesday Evenings

ROADMASTER *Custom Built by* BUICK

uick Roadmaster, 1954

adillac, 1953 ◀◀◀   Cadillac, 1953 ◀◀   Buick Roadmaster, 1954 ◀

You can make your "someday" come true now

YOU promised yourself, didn't you, that someday you would own a car that came up to your dreams?

That it would be a car of stature and distinction? That it would be luxuriously smooth and supremely able? That it would look and feel and perform the part of the car of a man at the top?

Well, sir—today can be that day.

For such a car is at hand now, more easily attainable than you may think. You see it pictured here, and the name is proudly spelled out on

each rear fender: ROADMASTER. It is custom production. Its appointment is subject to your individual taste. Its quality is the best that Buick builds. *Its price per pound is the lowest in the fine-car field.*

But apart from its impressive length and breadth and breath-taking beauty (it carries the world's newest body, with the panoramic visibility of Buick's famed sweep-back windshield)—this superb automobile is an automobile of supreme command.

When you drive it you will know that this is so.

When you call on ROADMASTER's magnificent V8 power, feel the smooth tranquility of Twin-Turbine Dynaflow, feather your way with the consummate ease of Safety Power Steering, sense the solid velvet of Buick's buoyant ride—then you will know that this is the car you always meant to own "someday."

So why wait? Call your Buick dealer today, or the first thing tomorrow. He'll gladly arrange a ROADMASTER demonstration and you can judge things from there.

BUICK Division of GENERAL MOTORS

ROADMASTER *Custom Built by* BUICK

Buick Roadmaster, 1954

87

Low...and behold! A new concept of low-cost motoring!

The Bel Air Sport Coupe—one of 14 new Fisher Body beauties in three new series.

the motoramic Chevrolet for 1955!

Here is excitement on wheels . . .

the newest, freshest thing you ever laid eyes on.

And it's even more exciting to drive

than to look at!

Take a good look and you'll know that the Motoramic Chevrolet is far more than just a new model. Take the wheel and you'll realize that it's more, even, than a completely new car!

For this is the Chevrolet that began with a whole new idea—the idea that a low-priced car can be made to look, ride and perform like the very finest and highest-priced automobiles.

Big order? You bet! So big that only the world's leading car builders could have filled it. Chevrolet and General Motors alone have the resources and the facilities it takes to put this great new idea on wheels.

Everything's new in the Motoramic Chevrolet—from its tubeless tires to its lower top! Your Chevrolet dealer will be happy to show it to you. . . . Chevrolet Division of General Motors, Detroit 2, Michigan.

GREAT NEW V8—TWO NEW 6's! New "Turbo-Fire V8" delivers 162 h.p. with an ultra-high compression ratio of 8 to 1. Two new 6's, too—the new "Blue-Flame 136" with Powerglide (optional at extra cost) and the new "Blue-Flame 123."

SWEEP-SIGHT WINDSHIELD WITH FOUR-FENDER VISIBILITY! Chevrolet's new Sweep-Sight Windshield curves around to vertical corner pillars. And you can see all four fenders from the driver's seat!

OVERDRIVE JOINS THE POWER TEAMS! Take your choice. There's new Overdrive teamed with the new V8 or the new "Blue-Flame 123." There's Powerglide teamed with the

new V8 or the new "Blue-Flame 136." (Powerglide and Overdrive are extra-cost options.) And there's a new standard transmission teamed with the new V8 or the "Blue-Flame 123."

WONDERFUL NEW GLIDE-RIDE FRONT SUSPENSION! New spherical joints flex freely to cushion road shocks. New Anti-Dive Braking Control, exclusive with Chevrolet, assures "heads up" stops.

A VENTILATING SYSTEM THAT REALLY WORKS! Chevrolet's new High-Level Ventilating System takes in air at hood-high level, away from road heat, fumes and dust.

NEW OUTRIGGER REAR SPRINGS! Rear springs are longer—and they're

attached at the outside of the frame to give you greater stability in cornering.

EVEN AIR CONDITIONING, IF YOU WISH! Air is heated or cooled by a single highly efficient unit. This is only one of the wonderful extra-cost options you can get!

MORE THAN A NEW CAR . . .

A NEW CONCEPT OF LOW-COST MOTORING

Chevrolet

Chevrolet, 1955

The sports-car styled 1954 Buick SPECIAL Convertible—lowest-priced of Buick's four great [...] now V8 powered for record-high performance, compression ratio, fuel e[...]

Thing of beauty and a joy for budgets

STUDY this one well, good friend — then ready yourself for the high-voltage news.

This automobile—this gorgeous grace of glass and color and flowing line pictured here — is the 1954 Buick SPECIAL Convertible.

It is Buick's lowest-priced Convertible.

It sells for just a few dollars more than similar models of the so-called "low-price three."

But from that point on, it differs every step of the way.

It's styled to the breath of Spring and the lift of a breeze.

It's pulsed with a completely new V8 that's in the record books as the highest-powered engine ever placed in a Buick of this budget-priced Series.

It's cradled on a chassis of 122 inches, where four coil springs, and a steadying torque-tube, and a sensational new front-end geometry give you a ride and handling ease that come pretty near to bliss.

And it's new, this Buick—completely new, like every 1954 Buick.

New in style, body, interior. New in the backswept expanse of its panoramic windshield. New in the wider swing-open of its doors. New in the better fuel economy of its Power-Head Pistons. New in a long list of advancements that add to comfort, convenience and safety.

Your Buick dealer cordially invites you to drop in and see this stunning new Buick and judge for yourself what a thrill and a buy it is in every way.

BUICK *Division of* GENERAL MOTORS

When better automobiles are built Buick will build them

BUICK
the Beautiful Buy

Buick, 1954

Dollar for Dollar

You Can't Beat a

PONTIAC

STAR CHIEF CONVERTIBLE

A General Motors Masterpiece

National Open Champion!

Here is the car that is sparking the new trend to convertibles—that long, low Silver Streaked style-setter up above. And here's what makes it the all-out favorite of roving, sun-loving Americans from coast to coast.

In the Pontiac manner, this rakish beauty offers more smart distinction, more tasteful luxury, more spacious comfort and more dashing

performance than a like amount of money ever covered before.

And that phrase applies without a change to every other Pontiac model. The prideful satisfaction of impressive size and beauty . . . the ever-new thrill of abundant, surging power . . . the happy confidence inspired by unquestioned dependability—*all* the special qualities of

fine-car ownership are yours in a Pontiac. Yet the price of this distinguished car is within a few dollars of the very lowest on any new car!

Drop in for a test of Pontiac's great all-around performance, and check on the actual figure required to put a big, luxurious Silver Streak in your driveway. You can count on it—you will be delightfully surprised.

DON'T MISS DAVE GARROWAY'S NIGHTTIME SHOW—NBC-TV • PONTIAC MOTOR DIVISION OF GENERAL MOTORS CORPORATION

Cadillac FOR 1955

This is the most significant announcement in Cadillac history!

For it introduces to the world's motorists our greatest achievement in fifty-three years of motor car production—the 1955 Cadillac!

It is, beyond question, the most magnificent Cadillac of all time!

It is, as you can readily see, magnificent in beauty. Its new, jewel-like grille assembly . . . its new sculptured side treatment . . . its graceful new roof line . . . all add immeasurably to Cadillac's world-famous styling.

It is magnificent, too, in performance. There's a great new 250-h.p. engine . . . a refined Hydra-Matic Drive . . . advanced Cadillac Power Steering . . . and, as an option at extra cost, improved Cadillac Power Braking.

And it is magnificent in luxury. Its interiors are almost unbelievably beautiful . . . and each is offered in a wide selection of gorgeous new fabrics and leathers.

This, in summary, is the new Standard of the World—and it awaits your inspection now in your dealer's showroom. Stop in soon—for a personal appraisal of this Cadillac masterpiece.

The spectacular Eldorado—featuring a 270-h.p. Cadillac engine.

CADILLAC MOTOR CAR DIVISION • GENERAL MOTORS CORPO

The magnificent Cadillac Series Sixty Special—new masterwork of the industry's master craftsme.

Presents the Most Beautiful and Finest
Performing Cars in Its History !

The dramatic Cadillac Coupe de Ville—offering the most colorful and breath-taking interiors of all time.

The inspiring Cadillac Convertible—an exciting and brilliant expression of the new Cadillac styling.

What's up in styling? power?

New Safety. *When you want quick action to get out of a traffic tight-spot, you just push the accelerator pedal the last half inch beyond full throttle—and the way those variable pitch propellers in Dynaflow Drive go to work is hard to believe.*

rformance?

thrill of the year is Buick

OF COURSE there's a fresh, new-day note to its styling, from that gleaming Wide-Screen Grille to the smart sweep of that new tail assembly.

Of course there's new power beneath that graceful bonnet—a new high of 188 hp in the low-price SPECIAL — a new high of 236 hp in the CENTURY, SUPER and ROADMASTER.

But the big thrills go even deeper in these 1955 Buicks.

We took a tip from aeronautics

When we tell you these eager new Buicks use the modern airplane's principle of "variable pitch" propulsion, we mean that literally.

As any aeronautical engineer will tell you, one of the greatest boons to aviation has been a propeller that uses one "pitch" of its blades for take-off and fast climbing — another "pitch" for gas-saving in the cruising range.

*And now Buick engineers have applied this pitch-changing principle to Dynaflow Drive.**

A new sensation in driving

What happens when the little blades of the "stator" — deep inside a Dynaflow Drive — change their pitch like the blades of a plane propeller?

The answer is waiting for you now — in the handsomest, ablest and highest-powered Buicks that ever greeted a new year.

So what are you waiting for? Better get behind the wheel of a 1955 Buick—and be up to date on the greatest advance in years.

BUICK *Division of* GENERAL MOTORS

Standard on Roadmaster, optional at extra cost on other Series.

WHEN BETTER AUTOMOBILES ARE BUILT
BUICK WILL BUILD THEM

iles per gallon

ctacular new Dynaflow ment, added to other advances t years, gives you up to e miles per gallon than Buicks 1948.

and a new high in V8 power

236 hp in the ROADMASTER
236 hp in the SUPER
236 hp in the CENTURY
188 hp in the SPECIAL

STEEP HILL

American Motors Announce

NEW IDEA! *You never saw such luxury in a car priced so low. Genuine leathers and exquisite nylon jacquards, color-keyed from roof lining to two-tone carpet.*

NEW IDEA! *It's All-Season Air Conditioning*—greatest health, comfort, safety feature of fifty years. No cold in winter! No heat in summer! No traffic roar or dust—constant fresh, filtered air. Needs no trunk space. A Rambler so equipped costs less than an ordinary car!*

*Patents applied for

NEW IDEA! *You're cradled in deep, Airliner Reclining Seats that adjust to let you rest on the roughest roads. Make up into Twin Travel Beds in most models.*

New Idea! On Television: "Disneyland" . . . great new all-family entertainment, ABC Network, see TV listings for time, station.

JEWELRY BY VAN CLEEF & ARPELS · GOWNS BY CEIL CHAPMAN

You're LOOKING AT IT NOW—the *first* new car from dynamic American Motors!

Not just a new car, but a complete *new idea* in automobiles, to meet the new motoring wants of millions.

Here's the new idea in luxury . . . the rakish flair of the continental sports car, with color-smart interiors like you've never seen before!

Here's the new idea in performance. The liveliest, easiest-to-handle car you've ever had your hands on. A Rambler that darts through traffic . . . turns in the shortest radius, parks easier and out-maneuvers any sedan built in America today . . . and that out-distances them all on a tankful of gasoline!

Here are whole new ideas in comfort and safety. *Complete* "All-Season" Air Conditioning* Airliner Reclining Seats. A new kind of Deep Coil Ride that smooths out the bumps as it hugs the road. A new kind of safety construction . . . Double Strength Unit Body.

See and try this newest idea in automobiles—for never before has a car so fine *been priced so low.* Now on display at all Hudson Dealers and Nash Dealers throughout America.

NEW IDEA in "*get up and go*" . . . *smart as tomorrow from its rakish sports car grille to its dashing continental rear tire mount, the new Rambler is easiest to handle in city traffic and on the highway.*

Whole **New Idea** in Automobiles

It's the Country
Club in Coral and
Snowberry White! *One of
Rambler's 22 rainbow-gay color
combinations—in smart sedans,
hardtop convertibles, station wagons.*

NEW IDEA! *Here's spectacular
performance in a car that turns in
38-foot circle. Unique, new Deep
Coil Ride keeps you grooved to curves.
Pictured here is the Rambler "Cross
Country"—the New Idea in station wagons.*

THE 1955

Rambler

American Motors Corporation, Detroit, Michigan

NOW AT ***Nash*** DEALERS AND HUDSON DEALERS EVERYWHERE

▶ *Buick Roadmaster, 1955*

In the market for a car that's sweet, smooth, and sassy?

Chevy's got 20 to pick from

Here's the whole beautiful line-up of '57 Chevrolets. And every last one — from the "One-Fifty" 2-Door Sedan to the dashing new Corvette — brings you a special, spirited way of going that's Chevy's alone!

The "One-Fifty" Utility Sedan.
The "Two-Ten" Beauville.
The "Two-Ten" Townsman.
The "Two-Ten" 4-Door Sedan.
The "One-Fifty" 2-Door Sedan.
The Bel Air 4-Door Sedan.
The "Two-Ten" Sport Sedan.
The "One-Fifty" Handyman.
The "Two-Ten" 2-Door Sedan.
The "One-Fifty" 4-Door Sedan.
The Bel Air Nomad.
The "Two-Ten" Sport Coupe.
The Bel Air Convertible.

14. The Bel Air 2-Door Sedan.
15. The "Two-Ten" Handyman.
16. The "Two-Ten" Delray Club Coupe.
17. The Corvette Sports Car.
18. The Bel Air Sport Sedan.
19. The Bel Air Sport Coupe.
20. The Bel Air Townsman.

See your favorite "number" at your Chevrolet dealer's. . . . Chevrolet Division of General Motors, Detroit 2, Michigan.

CHEVROLET

1 USA

'57 CHEVROLET

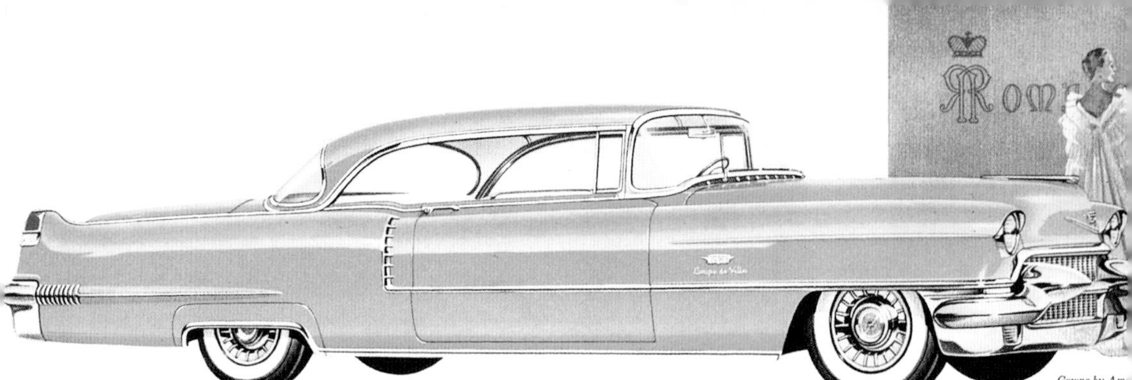

Gowns by Ame

Owners tell us that one of the most rewarding aspects of Cadillac ownership is the remarkable *friendliness* which they encounter at the wheel. Wherever they travel, they find that the "car of cars" introduces them in a very special manner—and seems to inspire the confidence and respect of those about them. This unique Cadillac virtue comes, of course, as something extra when you make your decision for Cadillac. It comes in addition to the car's great beauty—its outstanding performance—and its marvelous comfort and handling ease. We suggest that you visit your dealer soon for a personal appraisal of this glorious list of Cadillac virtues—and to learn why this is such a wonderful season to make the move, both for delivery and economy. CADILLAC MOTOR CAR DIVISION • GENERAL MOTORS CORPORATION

Cadillac

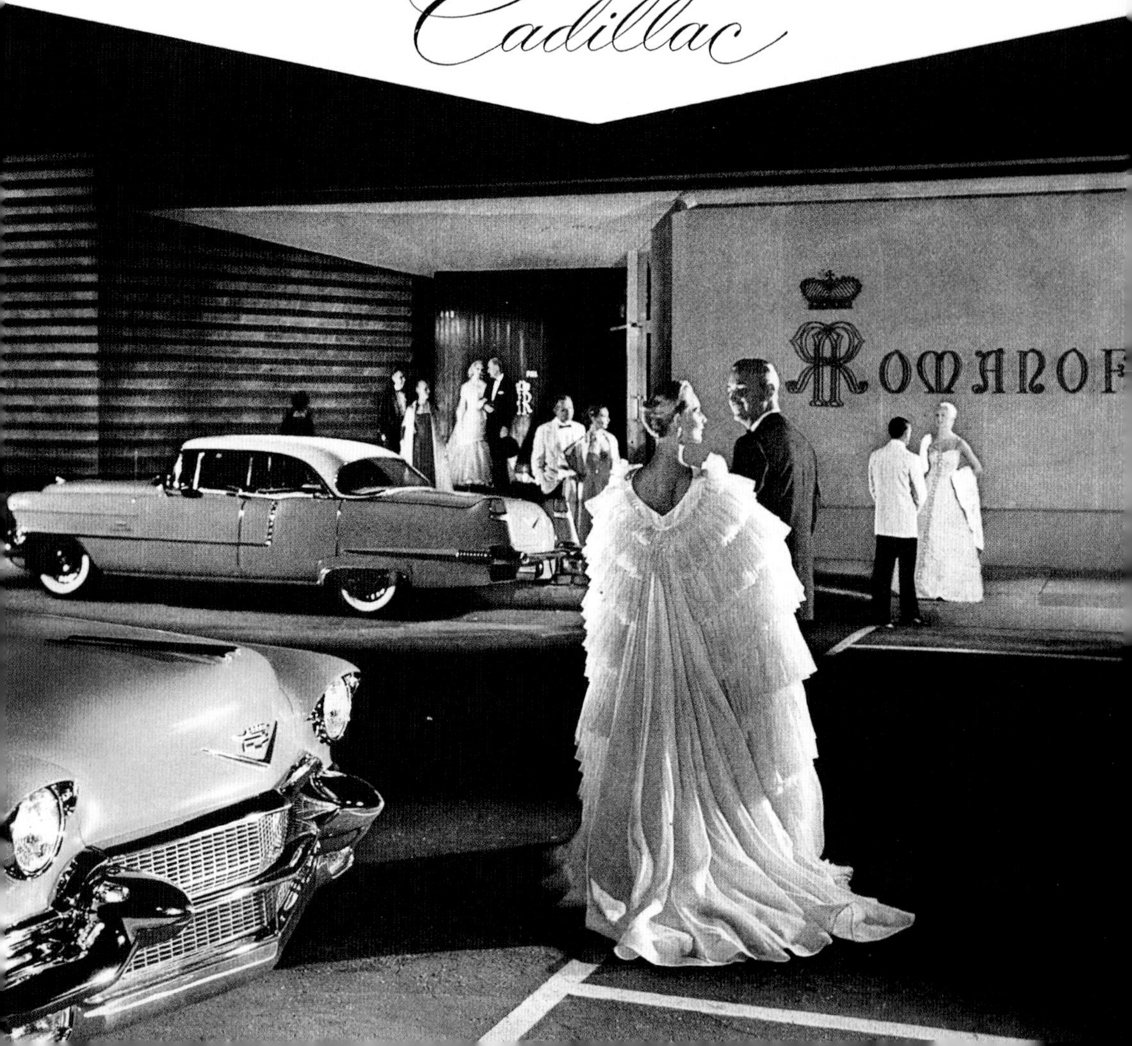

It Gives a Man a New Outlook...

...when he first views the world through the windshield of his own Cadillac car. In fact, we have it on the word of Cadillac owners themselves that it constitutes one of the most edifying experiences of a motorist's life. There is, for instance, the wholly new sense of pride he feels as he sits in possession of a motor car that is so widely respected and admired. There is the entirely new feeling of confidence and mastery he enjoys as he puts the car through its brilliant paces for the very first time. There is the priceless satisfaction of knowing that he is surrounded by every luxury and safeguard known to automotive science. And, finally, there is his deep inner pleasure in realizing that he has made one of motordom's soundest investments. And, of course, these wonderful sentiments will be all the more pronounced for the lucky motorist who makes the move to Cadillac in 1957. Why not visit your dealer for a preview journey and see for yourself? You're welcome to try the view from the driver's seat at any time. CADILLAC MOTOR CAR DIVISION • GENERAL MOTORS CORPORATION

Chevrolet, 1957 ◀◀   Cadillac, 1956 ◀   Cadillac, 1956

As you would expect, it's Oldsmobile—pioneer in hardtop styling—that brings you the *first luxury hardtop with four doors.*

This Ninety-Eight DeLuxe Holiday Sedan is smart as a convertible, yet offers full four-door sedan convenience *and room.* No center posts mar the flow of lines—and there's no folding the front seat forward ever! From the smallest detail right on to the challenging performance of the "Rocket" 202 Engine, this is a car for the person who favors the exceptional. Come try it at your Oldsmobile dealer's . . . now!

NINETY-EIGHT DELUXE
HOLIDAY SEDAN

Oldsmobile, 1955

Star Chief Four-door Catalina

Born to Go Together!

STRATO-STREAK V-8

+

STRATO-FLIGHT HYDRA-MATIC

Wheeling this big beauty down the road you're in command of a *very special* kind of performance—performance reserved exclusively for the pleasure of Pontiac owners!

Why so special? Well, first of all, under that broad, gleaming hood there's the industry's most advanced high-torque, high-compression engine—the brilliant new 227-h.p. Strato-Streak V-8. Most cars would be satisfied to stop right there—but not Pontiac! A new transmission was developed to refine all that

power—and refined it is, with the oil-smooth Strato-Flight Hydra-Matic*, tailor-made for Strato-Streak power—*and nothing else!*

The result? America's newest, smoothest, most modern performance team and *the greatest "go" on wheels!*

Why not come in and take up our invitation to try it? And don't hesitate to ask about prices. When you do, we're betting you and Pontiac will be going steady! *An extra-cost option

SEE YOUR PONTIAC DEALER

You can actually buy a big, glamorous Pontiac 860 for less than you would pay for 43 models of the low-priced three!

The '56 Strato-Streak

PONTIAC

WITH STRATO-FLIGHT HYDRA-MATIC

The Most Sweeping

Pontiac has it in th

OVER SIX DOZEN "FIRSTS", INCLUDING...

STAR FLIGHT BODY DESIGN—*a Pontiac Exclusive—longer and lower than ever before— the year's most distinctive new automotive styling.*

THE "OFF THE SHOULDER" LOOK INTERIOR STYLING—*a fashion "first" for '57—perfectly color-matched with the exterior of your choice.*

NEW WORLD-RECORD V-8 ENGINE—*270 h.p. in Star Chief and Super Chief, 252 h.p. in the Chieftain— with smoother Strato-Flight Hydra-Matic.*

CLOUD-SOFT, LEVEL-LINE RIDE—*the ride sensation of the year—a new suspension system based on a big, road-hugging 124- or 122-inch wheelbase.*

THREE NEW BODY-PRICED SERIES: STAR CHIEF • SUPER CHIEF • CHIEFTA

Change of All!

Surprise Package of '57!

e boldest new-car move of the year, Pontiac for '57 leaves them all
d—in beauty, in performance, in ride!

Here's the year's most clear-cut break with the commonplace. It's
sh, new styling story told in crisp, dramatic lines—giving the cue
trend that's sure to follow!

And its newness goes all the way through: Brand-new power even
efficient than its predecessor that broke over 50 stock car records
ed all eights in miles per gallon . . . Strato-Flight Hydra-Matic*
nothing short of perfection . . . new suspension ideas and pre-

cision handling that crack the whip over the wildest roads imaginable.
And it comes to you proved as no other car in history, because a proto-
type of this big, eye-opening dazzler strutted its easy way through
100,000 miles of the most rugged road tests the engineers could devise!

Be among the first to bring yourself up to date on the car that
caught them all napping.

Drive this '57 Pontiac and sample in a single memorable mile all
that's been proved by 100,000 miles of testing! *An extra-cost option*

PONTIAC MOTOR DIVISION OF GENERAL MOTORS CORPORATION

IT'S AMERICA' NUMBER ① ROAD CAR!

WHO SAYS TOMORROW NEVER COMES?

Don't miss Plymouth's two great new TV programs: "The Lawrence Welk Show" and "The Ray Anthony Show."

YOU'RE LOOKING AT IT!

This is the car you might have expected in 1960, yet it's here today—the *only* car that dares to break the time barrier.

Plymouth has reached far into the future to bring you 1960-new Flight-Sweep Styling, and a *car-full* of exciting features . . . revolutionary new Torsion-Aire ride . . . terrific new power for safety with the fabulous Fury "301" V-8 engine, super-powered to 235 hp . . . super-safe Total Contact Brakes . . . exhilarating sports-car handling.

1960 is as near as your Plymouth dealer. Drive this *great* automobile *today!*

SUDDENLY, IT'S 1960 ➤ PLYMOUTH

Cadillac presents

the greatest advancements it has ever achieved

in motor car styling and engineering ! ➤➤➤

The Sixty Special

Cadillac for 1957...brillia[

Embodied in the beautiful cars on these pages are the most important and most significant automotive advancements we have ever been privileged to present to the motoring public.

Entirely new in design and engineering, and bringing to the world's highways a wholly new standard of quality and excellence—Cadillac for 1957 represents one of the greatest achievements of all time.

Cadillac's renowned stylists have created a brilliant new type of

beauty . . . majestically graceful in every line and contour . . . w fully exciting in spirit and in concept . . . and with a dramatical balance of chrome and glass and steel.

Cadillac's master coachcrafters have brought a new meas luxury and excitement to the car's interiors . . . with gorgeou fabrics and leathers . . . with inspiring new colors and patterns . with marvelous new appointments and conveniences on every

Cadillac, 1956

w in beauty, brilliantly new in performance!

The Eldorado Biarritz

nd Cadillac's world-famous engineers have introduced a sensa-
new concept of automotive performance ... with two great new
lac engines ... with an even smoother, more responsive Hydra-
 Drive ... with greatly improved power steering and power brak-
 with a revolutionary new frame design ... and with a host of
 equally vital engineering advancements.

hese dramatic Cadillac achievements are being presented for 1957

in ten individual body styles, including the breath-taking Eldorado
series. Each is a Cadillac masterpiece ... a brilliant tribute to the men
who design and build the Standard of the World.

We extend you our cordial invitation to see ... to inspect ... and
to drive the new 1957 Cadillac at your very earliest convenience.

It will be the most enlightening experience of your motoring life.

★ YOUR CADILLAC DEALER ★

There Are Some Secrets a Man Can't Keep ...

...when he is seen in the driver's seat of a new 1957 Cadillac. And not the least among these is the fact that he is a man of unusual practical wisdom. For it is widely recognized that when a motorist selects the "car of cars", he selects one of the soundest of all motor car purchases. The original cost of a new Cadillac, for instance, is remarkably modest—in view of the great beauty and luxury and performance it represents. Cadillac's marvelous economy of operation and its extraordinary dependability are without counterpart on the world's highways. And Cadillac's unsurpassed resale value assures its owner a greater return on his investment than any other automobile in the land. If you would like to enjoy these many practical benefits in *your* next motor car—then you are looking for Cadillac! The car is waiting for you in your dealer's showroom—and this is the perfect moment to make the move quickly and economically. CADILLAC MOTOR CAR DIVISION • GENERAL MOTORS CORPORATION

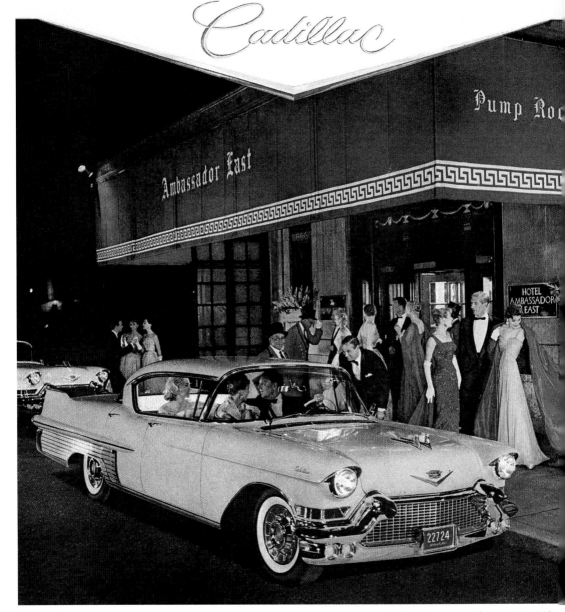

Cadillac, 1956

▶ *Buick, 1959*　▶ ▶ *Imperial, 1956*　▶ ▶ ▶ *Buick, 1959*

THERE'S NOTHING LIKE A NEW CAR . . . AND NOTHING LIKE THE '60 BUICK LE SABRE 4-DOOR SEDAN YOU SEE HERE.

BUICK'S ALL-TIME BEST

There is more than mechanical excellence behind the greatness of this Buick. There is more than the Buick brakes, unsurpassed on any American car today. There is more than the smoothest automatic transmission made. More than the wonderful silence of this car in motion. More than the room, and the solid, confident feeling of an important and wholly road-worthy automobile.

More than all these is the deep-down satisfaction you get from the fact that this car's name is BUICK . . . and everybody knows what that stands for.

BUICK MOTOR DIVISION, GENERAL MOTORS CORPORATION

THE TURBINE DRIVE BUICK '60

BUICK LeSABRE—The lowest-priced Buick   **BUICK INVICTA**—The high-performance Buick   **BUICK ELECTRA**—The finest Buick of all

FIRST BIG FAMILY CAR —
WITH A SPORTS CAR HEA

It's big, bold, buoyant

THE AIR BORI

STRETCH OUT IN LOUNGE-CAR COMFORT—Immaculately tailored seats are more than 5 feet wide and sofa-soft. Headroom, hiproom, legroom and footroom for all 6 riders, including those n the middle.

THRILL TO THE B-12000 ENGINE—Most advanced V8 yet. 12,000 pounds of thrust behind every power strok nodal-point mounting and center-of-percussion balance fo ness, sweetness, silence.

Picture a cruiser that's nimble as a PT boat.

A bomber deft as a jet fighter.

Picture a big and spacious automobile with the heart and soul, the sparkle and spirit, the control, obedience, response and maneuverability of the sportiest sports car ever.

We're talking about the bold and buoyant Buick for '58 —and until you drive it you don't know what driving is.

For here in this straight-from-tomorrow Buick you boss a B-12000 engine as modern as the look of the car itself.

Here, behind this fresh face of fashion, you pilot a Flight Pitch Dynaflow* literally born of aircraft design.

Here, in this fabulous B-58 Buick you glide, soar, float— with a Miracle Ride plus Buick's Air-Poise Suspension.*

Here, in brief, you discover totally new concepts in driving delight—extending from noise and vibration suppression to ingeniously air-cooled aluminum brakes*...

Because this, you discover, is a car born of more aircraft principles—including greater use of aluminum —than any other car yet built...

This, you finally realize, is the first big car that's really light on its feet.

There's a Buick — a roomy and radiant B-58 Buick — ready at your Buick dealer's—*today.*

Drive it and give the red-blooded *you* a break.

BUICK *Division of* GENERAL MOTORS

Flight Pitch Dynaflow standard on LIMITED and ROADMASTER 75, optional at extra cost on other Series. Air-Poise Suspension optional at extra cost on all Series. Aluminum Front Brakes standard on all Series except SPECIAL. Safety-Buzzer standard on LIMITED and ROADMASTER 75, optional at extra cost on other Series.

See TALES OF WELLS FARGO, Monday Nights, NBC
and THE PATRICE MUNSEL SHOW, Friday Nights, A

When better automobiles are built Buick will

 **B-58 BUICK**

TINGLE TO FLIGHT PITCH DYNAFLOW—"Low" is replaced by automatic downhill engine braking. "Drive" gives you the astonshing performance of triple turbines plus "a million ways to switch the pitch."

ENJOY IT ALL TO THE HILT with the one and only Safety-Buzzer.* Decide on a safe, sane miles-per-hour. R figure to view in the "window." If you exceed that pace—buz Drop below it and the buzzing stops.

A BOLD NEW CAR FOR A BOLD NEW GENERATION

PONTIAC

Lukens Steel Company ◄   *Pontiac, 1958*

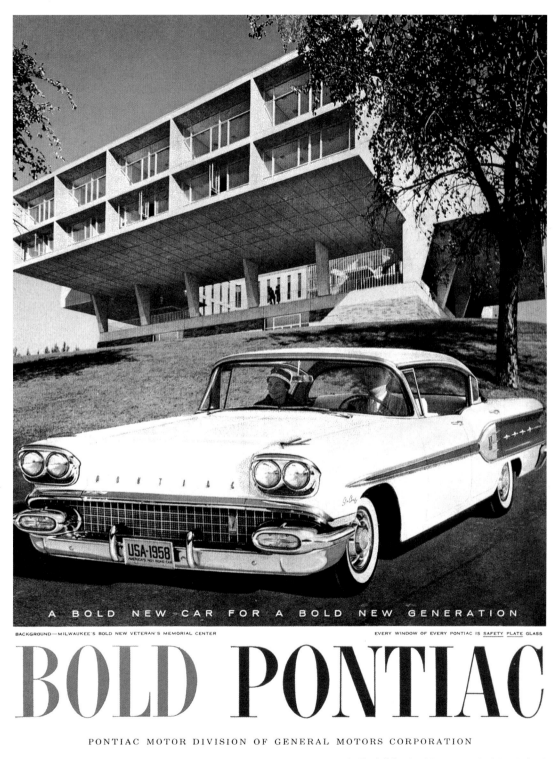

A BOLD NEW CAR FOR A BOLD NEW GENERATION

BACKGROUND—MILWAUKEE'S BOLD NEW VETERAN'S MEMORIAL CENTER

EVERY WINDOW OF EVERY PONTIAC IS SAFETY PLATE GLASS

BOLD PONTIAC

PONTIAC MOTOR DIVISION OF GENERAL MOTORS CORPORATION

Pontiac, 1956   ▶ Thunderbird, 1958   ▶▶ Mercury, 1958   ▶▶▶ Ford, 1958

*America's most individual car—an automotive
jewel that's pure Thunderbird in design,
spirit and performance...with full fine-car
room, comfort and luxury for four*

ew version of a great classic…the <u>4-passenger</u>

NDERBIRD

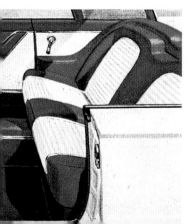

Another first from Ford! In the 1958 Thunderbird, Ford has created a wholly new size and type of fine car. It gives you Thunderbird compactness, Thunderbird handling and traditional Thunderbird performance — yet, miraculously, it now gives you full fine-car room and comfort for *four* people! It brings you interior appointments that are unbelievably imaginative and luxurious. Now, happily, you can share your Thunderbird thrills with deserving friends. Now it's *twice the fun* to own the car that became an American classic the very day it was introduced. For details about America's most excitingly different car,

turn the page, please

FIRST STATION WAGONS TO COMBI

Mercury gives you superior performance in station wagons. You get new Marauder engines with as much as 330 hp — 4450 pounds of solid, road-hugging luxury — all wrapped up in Clean Line Modern Styling.

NOW YOU CAN ENJOY STATION-WAGON TRAVEL. This Mercury set out to give you station wagons that would as easily as passenger cars. And the results actually bea other car you could name. You get a 312- or 330-hp Mar V-8 — either one with brand-new Cool-Power Design. that means a new high in efficiency and economy — a new of response and maneuverability never before achiev a station wagon.

You move safely past trucks — enter fast-moving with an effortless ease that tops any passenger car Mercury. And there are dozens of wonderful new drivin like the push-button magic of Merc-O-Matic Keyboard Co

The magnificent Colony Park (*foreground*), the luxurious Voyager (*left*), the value-leading Commuter (*top right*)— Mercury's 3 series. Your choice of 6 models.

PIRITED PERFORMANCE WITH BEAUTY AND SIZE

YOU TRAVEL IN STYLE! Clean Line Modern Styling,
ry's reflection of the taste and tempo of our times. Lines as
as a bridge—free from useless chrome or wings or things.
like all good modern design, it's supremely functional.
ry, spacious hardtop design gives you the widest, most
rful view on wheels. There's no liftgate to get in the
hen loading; a rear window that disappears into the
e takes its place. And any Big M station wagon for 1958
you the largest, most usable cargo area you can find—
in all the dimensions that count.

wonder Big M station wagons lead their field in sales. We
you to see *all* the reasons at your Mercury dealer's.

1958 MERCURY

MEANS THE MOST FOR YOUR MONEY

Married in style and luxury! The 59 Thunderbird and the new Ford Galaxie

ANNOUNCING — TH

Brilliant wedding of Thunderbird elegance and
the world's most beautifully proportioned cars

The 59 Fords awarded the Gold Medal
of the Comité Français de L'Élégance
for beautiful proportions
at the Brussels World's Fair.

Just married in style to the Thunderbird!
smartest, richest and most exciting of 59 Fords—
gant new Galaxie. A bright new personality
and more! The Galaxie is a full "fine car" 6-passe
pression of Thunderbird grace—spirit—style an
in an altogether-new line of Fords.

It's Thunderbird in looks! The Galaxie, a
quickly see, is as wonderfully all-the-way Thu
as a low-priced Ford can be. The smart stra

NEW FORD *Galaxie*

roof and dramatic see-it-all rear window say
rbird *unmistakably*. So do the clean, crisp, low-
ody lines. Here is the most perfect match yet of
nderbird's silhouette—the most modern and most
"new look" in cars today!

under bird in luxury! New Galaxie appoint-
-like the plush, deep-pile carpets—are so very
rbird in taste. And just like the Thunderbird, the
seats you in the tailored elegance of specially

quilted and pleated fabrics. There's Thunderbird V-8
power, too. A surpassing luxury that tells you how
superbly these newlyweds "GO" together.

Reception now—you are invited. Why not come in
—this very week—see the new Galaxie and all the members of the year's most beautiful wedding. The experience, we bet, will please you proud. It might even set
you to planning a second honeymoon—most elegantly—
in the car that's Thunderbird in everything *except price!*

Reception
starting this week
at your
Ford Dealer's

SUPREMACY

In no other field of commerce has a single product stood so pre-eminently alone—for so long a time—as has the Cadillac car. For more than half a century, its name has been a living symbol of automotive goodness. And the Cadillac of 1958 has underscored this supremacy with revealing emphasis. To inspect it is to behold a motor car of incredible beauty. To drive it is to command the very finest in automotive performance. And to own it is to possess the most rewarding of personal possessions. This is a wonderful time to do all three—and your dealer is waiting with details on each of Cadillac's Fleetwood-crafted models, including the Eldorado Brougham.

Every Window of Every Cadillac is <u>Safety Plate</u> Glass • Gown by Henri Bendel

CADILLAC MOTOR CAR DIVISION • GENERAL MOTORS CORPORATION

Cadillac, 1958

Announcing
THE MARK IV
Continental

The fourth and finest in the Distinguished Series of the world's most admired car. LINCOLN DIVISION · FORD MOTOR COMPANY

Mark IV Continental, 1958

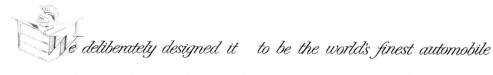

We deliberately designed it   to be the world's finest automobile

Beyond a doubt, this newest of fine cars goes well beyond the familiar concepts of luxury and performance. Indeed, that was our goal in creating the LIMITED. Thus, its interior presents a degree of elegance and comfort that sets a new level of magnificence. Its performance exceeds existing standards—to the point of providing a wholly new experience in ease of handling and serenity of ride. Even in the matter of its extra length, the LIMITED goes beyond the call of familiar dimensions. You will find this superbly crafted automobile a most satisfying possession—and your Buick dealer will be understandably proud to introduce you to it.

BUICK *Division of* GENERAL MOTORS

PROUDLY PRESENTED, PROUDLY POSSESSED— *The*

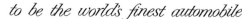

LIMITED

Buick, 1958

Now there's a full series of elegant Impalas, including the new Sport Sedan shown here.

ALL NEW ALL OVER AGAIN!

It's shaped to the new American taste with a lean, clean silhouette, crisp new contours, beautifully restrained accents. It brings you more spaciousness and comfort with a new Body by Fisher. It has a bright new sheen—a new kind of finish that keeps its luster without waxing for up to three years. New bigger brakes. Vast new areas of visibility. New Hi-Thrift 6. New handling ease and road steadiness. It's new right down to the tires!

Never before has an automobile manufacture made such sweeping changes two years in a row. And never before has any car been new like this one.

The 1959 Chevrolet is your kind of car. Shaped to reward your new taste in style. Designed to anticipate your desire for greater roominess and comfort. Engineered to bring you greater safety, economy, ease of handling and smoothness of ride.

Chevrolet's new Slimline design brings entirely new poise and proportion to automobile styling. Inside the new and roomier Body by Fisher you'll find truly tasteful elegance. And you'll be more through the new Vista-Panoramic windshield that curves overhead. It's more than 50 per cent larger!

There's much, much more. A new steering ratio makes handling easier. New suspension engineering gives

you a more stable ride. (Level Air suspension* is now even softer!) There's a sweet new edition of Turboglide*. A new Hi-Thrift 6 that goes and goes on a gallon. New Safety-Master brakes. And with all that's new, you'll find those fine old Chevrolet virtues of economy and practicality. See this fresh new Chevy at your Chevrolet dealer's. . . Chevrolet Division of General Motors, Detroit 2, Michigan.

*Optional at extra cost

CHEVROLET

What America wants, America gets in a Chevy!

'59 CHEVROLET

The new Bel Air 4-Door Sedan—like all '59 Chevies—rides no stronger, rides Types cord tires.

Chevrolet, 1959

The Lincoln Premiere Landau

MOST DRAMATIC DEBUT OF 1959:
NEWEST EDITION OF THE LINCOLN LOOK

A masterpiece at rest... A miracle in motion

This is the Lincoln for 1959. The lineage of its glorious past is apparent—struck beautifully into metal and glass. But there is more, much more, to see, to feel, to behold.

Here, indeed, is the timeless Lincoln look. And, this *look* is just one reason why Lincoln is such a practical investment now, and worth so much more for all the years ahead. It is reassuring, as well, to know that Lincoln shares its appearance and dimensions with no other motorcar.

Of all the 1959 cars, Lincoln is the widest, deepest and most comfortable inside—unquestionably the most handsomely appointed. And Lincoln, powered by America's most agile engine, handles with incredible ease.

What's more its unique uniframe construction brings a new stability, safety and silence to motoring. If you yearn for the distinctive, yet wish to invest shrewdly, the Lincoln must inevitably be your motorcar choice for 1959.

The Lincoln lines are completely original—unshared with any other car.

THE 1959
LINCOLN LOOK

*Classic beauty—
unexcelled craftsmanship.*

LINCOLN DIVISION • FORD MOTOR COMPANY

coln, 1959

▶ *Imperial, 1959*   ▶▶ *Mobilgas, 1950*

Presenting ... the NEW 1959

IMPERIAL

... excellence without equal

The 1959 Imperial LeBaron Silvercrest four door hardtop . . . fresh from Imperial's all-new plant to host this year's Imperial Ball

Today, America has a new measurement for excellence in motoring.

IMPERIAL FOR 1959 . . . a car whose great dignity is matched by an eagerness of spirit . . . whose luxury and elegance are made richer by a gracious practicality.

A car in which careful interior redesign has provided more space for passengers . . . a car which makes available for the first time front seats that swivel doorward to make entry and exit easy.

IMPERIAL FOR 1959 . . . a car whose farsighted engineering concepts combine spectacular handling ease with a firm sense of absolute control . . . whose newly designed engine develops enormous power with fewer engine revolutions . . . so it need never race or strain or raise its voice.

A car which can be equipped with Auto-Pilot, to remind you of the speed limit, and to maintain a steady turnpike pace, hour on hour, up hill and down, without a touch of the accelerator.

IMPERIAL FOR 1959 . . . whose spacious Royal Coach Body gives you new dimensions of comfort and enjoyment. A car that comes to you in all its carefully crafted excellence from America's newest automotive plant . . . designed for the utmost in quality control.

IMPERIAL FOR 1959 . . . excellence without equal. A boastful statement? The car is ready for your inspection at Imperial showrooms. See it. Drive it. And then decide.

ALL TANGLED UP IN GASOLINE CLAIMS?

HERE'S A TIP...

No other gasoline has yet equalled this power and mileage record—

22.3 MILES PER GALLON AVERAGE

IN THE 1953 Mobilgas Economy Run 25 new U.S. stock cars, using Mobilgas or Mobilgas Special, averaged an amazing 22.3 miles per gallon over a punishing 1206-mile route.

Proof!...it takes perfect balance of high volatility, high power and high mileage ingredients to deliver top economy and performance! Fill up at your Mobilgas dealer today!

Mobilgas
SOCONY-VACUUM

GET HIGH QUALITY ECONOMY GASOLINE

Mobilgas, 1953

Hatful of Pep!

AND in your car famous Fire-Chief is a
tankful of pep. Ready to give you quick starts . . .
fast warm-ups . . . smooth getaways.
Fire-Chief is *regular priced*, too. So step up
your driving pleasure. Fill up at your Texaco Dealer
. . . *the best friend your car ever had.*

TEXACO
FIRE-CHIEF
GASOLINE

THE TEXAS COMPANY
TEXACO DEALERS IN ALL 48 STATES
Texaco Products are also distributed in Canada and Latin America

TUNE IN: On television—the TEXACO STAR THEATER starring MILTON BERLE—every Tuesday night. On radio—
Metropolitan Opera Broadcasts—every Saturday afternoon. See newspaper for time and station.

Introducing...
From Sinclair's Space-Age Research

NEW 3-STAGE GASOLINE

OVER 100-OCTANE
NO INCREASE IN PRICE

New Sinclair Power-X Gives You 100-Octane Performance in All 3 Driving Stages

1 **STARTING** Power-primed with rocket fuel, new Power-X Gasoline is over 100-octane! You start quick as a click in any weather . . . and your engine warms up smooth and sweet. No stalling, no skipping.

2 **ACCELERATION** 12,000 pounds thrust at the touch of your toe! No need for fancy super-priced gasolines. With new Power-X, you get lightning getaway . . . reserve power for smoother, safer driving.

3 **MILEAGE** Those extra octanes mean extra economy, too . . . more miles in every thrifty gallon. And there's no increase in price! Watch for the new Power-X at your neighborhood Sinclair Dealer's Station.

NO PRICE INCREASE

SINCLAIR

WATCH FOR THE ARRIVAL OF NEW
POWER-X GASOLINE IN YOUR COMMUNITY

Sinclair Refining Company, 600 Fifth Avenue, New York 20, N. Y.

Sinclair, 1959

▶ *Diamond Chemica*

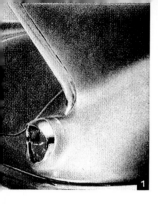

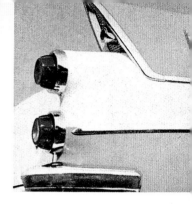

Diamond's Guide to Car Watching

(can you identify them?)*

Here are the southern exposures of nine northbound '57's. Dramatically different as these new cars are, they have one thing in common. On each is some chrome plating that started with DIAMOND Chromic Acid. DIAMOND ALKALI is one of the world's largest producers of chromium chemicals, and DIAMOND research has recently developed a new additive for chrome platers which reduces plating time and cost, gives a harder, brighter finish.

Progress like this helps explain why DIAMOND'S "Chemicals you live by" are preferred by so many industries, found in so many places.

DIAMOND ALKALI COMPANY, Cleveland 14, Ohio.

Diamond Chemicals

Your engine makes this much Acid every day

... And it's Acid Action—not friction— that causes 90% of engine wear

New Alkaline Shell X-100 Motor Oil counteracts Acid Action

If you are a typical motorist, in a normal day's driving:—a pint or more of acid is formed and passes through your car's engine, and it's acid action, not friction, that causes 90% of your engine wear. To neutralize the harmful effect of this acid, Shell Research has produced an alkaline motor oil—Shell X-100. Fortified with alkaline "X" safety factors, it neutralizes the acid action, prolonging the life of your engine.

The new Shell X-100 is a Premium Motor Oil. It is a Heavy Duty Motor Oil. In addition, it contains positive cleansing factors that help protect hydraulic valve lifters and other vital parts from fouling deposits.

Shell X-100 is the finest motor oil money can buy. Let your Shell dealer give your engine the protection of this new alkaline Shell X-100 Motor Oil today.

It's Incomparable!

ell Motor Oil, 1951 ◄ Shell Motor Oil, 1952

This is the Eldorado—a new adventure in automotive design and engineering—with brilliant and dramatic styling . . . hand-crafted, imported leather interiors . . . "disappearing" top . . . and a sensational 270-h.p. engine. In all that it is, and does, and represents . . . it is the finest fruit of Cadillac's never-ending crusade to build greater quality into the American motor car.

Now in limited production   •   Price on request

Eldorado

BY CADILLAC

They'll know you've *arrived*

when you drive up in an Edsel

Step into an Edsel and you'll learn where the excitement is this year.

Other drivers spot that classic vertical grille a block away—and never fail to take a long look at this year's most exciting car.

On the open road, your Edsel is watched eagerly for its already-famous performance.

And parked in front of your home, your Edsel always gets even more attention—because it always says a lot about you. It says you chose elegant styling, luxurious comfort and such exclusive features as Edsel's famous Teletouch Drive—only shift that puts the buttons where they belong, on the steering-wheel hub.

Your Edsel also means you made a wonderful buy. For of all medium-priced cars, this one really new car is actually priced the lowest.* See your Edsel Dealer this week.

Based on comparison of suggested retail delivered prices of the Edsel Ranger and similarly equipped cars in the medium-price field.

Above: Edsel Citation 2-door Hardtop. Engine: the E-475, with 10.5 to one compression ratio, 345 hp, 475 ft.-lb. torque. Transmission: Automatic with Teletouch Drive. Suspension: Ball-joint with optional air suspension. Brakes: self-adjusting.

EDSEL DIVISION · FORD MOTOR COMPANY

1958 EDSEL

Of all medium-priced cars, the one that's really new is the lowest-priced, too!

Cadillac Eldorado   Edsel, 1958

Consumer Products
144

BAUSCH & LOMB BALOMATIC

the slide projector with **HIGH** **PICTURE** **FIDELITY**

Always stays in focus...runs by itself!

Now Bausch & Lomb gives you *High Picture Fidelity*. Now you can project color slides with all the detail of the scenes you originally captured on film. The magic moments of your memories spring to life with full brilliance, astounding clarity and faithful color, just as high fidelity sound faithfully reproduces the beauty of great music. In addition, your slides *always stay in focus*, slide after slide after slide. No annoying slide "pop"...no fuzzy images. You have *true* automatic operation because you never have to get up to re-focus! Balomatic runs through your slide collection *all by itself*. You watch big, life-sized pictures, *not* the projector! Serve your guests refreshments...your slide show goes right along without you. Best relaxation a slide showman ever had!

The Balomatic—developed by world famous Bausch & Lomb optical scientists, creators of CinemaScope lenses and the finest optical instruments—*operates* just as beautifully as it *looks*. You project with 500-watt illumination; all controls grouped together on illuminated panel; 100% automatic with 4-to-60 second timing; finger-tip automatic and optional remote control; precise B & L Balcoted 5" lens; non-spill slide trays that store and protect 40 slides—35 mm, 828 and Super Slides in any kind of 2x2 mount.

Choose from three Balomatic models. Prices start at $84.50...available at low monthly terms. Your dealer is featuring *High Picture Fidelity* Balomatic today...visit him and see for yourself. Bausch & Lomb Optical Co., Rochester 2, New York.

BAUSCH & LOMB BALOMATIC

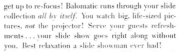

Wollensak, Electric Eye-Matic, 1953 ◄   *Bausch & Lomb Balomatic, 1958*   ► *Keystone,*

how much should you pay
for a fine 16mm movie camera?

Keystone K-51
16mm Magazine Movie Camera
with f2.5 coated lens
$139.50

Keystone K-56
16mm Magazine Turret
Movie Camera with ultra-fast
f1.9 coated lens
$189.50
(Telephoto lens optional at extra cost)

Keystone A-15
16mm Rollfilm Turret
Movie Camera with
ultra-fast f1.5 coated lens
$199.50
(Telephoto lens optional at extra cost)

photographed in Bermuda

Just the price of a Keystone . . . and no more. For no other camera at any price
ou finer results or better value. With Keystone, you get the clear, sharp detail
icture brilliance you have a right to expect . . . the precision engineering and simplicity
ation you have a right to demand. For versatility, ease and high-level performance,
look to Keystone 16mm movie cameras. Preferred by people
who can afford to pay more . . . but who know they don't have to.

K *Keystone*

REGISTERED IN YOUR NAME WITH A LIFETIME GUARANTEE

161M Magna-Scope Projector
screen from a distance of 20 feet. "Long-Throw"
a large rooms is optional. **$169.50**

View-Master 3-D adds DEPTH to pictures like this

"I'm clicking with 3-D* now!"

"The View-Master Personal Stereo Camera turned photography into an exciting adventure for me! There's nothing like the thrill you get out of taking and seeing beautiful color pictures of your family and friends in the amazing 'come to life' realism of View-Master 3-Dimension.

"And stereo pictures are so easy to take with the View-Master Personal Camera! People with little or no experience take excellent 3-D pictures the very first time …there's no focusing…no fussing with gadgets. Just one simple setting and snap the picture. It's that easy!

"But the most amazing thing is that the View-Master 3-D pictures actually cost less than black and white snapshots made with a box camera! These pictures can be viewed in View-Master Stereoscopes or projected in the new View-Master 'Stereo-matic' Projector. Before you buy *any* camera be sure to see the View-Master and the exciting 3-D pictures it takes."

View-Master Personal Stereo Camera … $149.00

VIEW-MASTER® Personal STEREO CAMERA

Write Sawyer's Inc., Box 490, Portland 7, Oregon, for free sample 3-D picture Reel.

THE NEW VIEW-MASTER *Stereo-matic* **500" 3-D PROJECTOR** For finest 3-Dimension projection. Ask your View-Master dealer for a demonstration. $177.50

Prices slightly higher in Canada
ⓒ Sawyer's Inc., Portland 7, Oregon
Trade Mark Reg. U. S. Pat. Off. Marca Registrada

DARKNESS MEANS… DANGER

PROTECT YOURSELF

Tonight .. be safe with an OLIN "Matched Pair" flashlight

NEW LOW PRICES
2-cell: only $1.35 less batteries
3-cell: only $1.55 less batteries
(For EXTRA RANGE and POWER)

$1.35 LESS BATTERIES

$1.55 LESS BATTERIES

BOND No. 102 Fresh SUPER POWER BATTERY

WINCHESTER No 1511 Fresh HI-POWER Super BATTERY

Available only in

WINCHESTER and **BOND** lines

OF **OLIN** INDUSTRIES, INC., Electrical Division, New Haven 4, Conn.

View Master Stereo Camera, 1953

Winchester Batteries, 1950

▶ *Motorola,*

KING-SIZE Valentines open to more than a foot and a half wide. Ask for #100V592. Price, $1.00.

A NORCROSS VALENTINE...

says what's in your *heart* the *way* you *want* to say it. To be sentimental . . . or old-fashioned or serious—or just for fun—say it with Norcross Valentines!

Be sure to see the beautiful selection at your Norcross dealer's, especially the *exclusive* Norcross King-Size and Queen-Size cards, the best of all ways to say "Be My Valentine." Look for these famous cards displayed in their special racks.

No matter which you choose . . . Norcross Valentines always please. No matter who's your "Valentine" you'll find just the *right* greeting at your Norcross dealer's *now*.

NORCROSS VALENTINES

Say the things you want to say

QUEEN-SIZE Valentines, half as large as King-Size (at half the price!). Ask for #50V538 and #50V338 Each 50 cents.

Mary had a little friend
Besides the lamb you know.
And everywhere that Mary went
This other friend would go.

She carried it to class each day
Along with books and rule.
And so did all the other kids
Who went to Mary's school.

At home, she saw it all the time
For it was loved by Mother.
And Daddy's office had it, too,
For he would use no other.

Ticonderoga is this friend,
A Pencil without master.
Its rounded edges, *LeadFast* point,
Make writing smoother, faster.

Ticonderoga's famous name
Is doubly exciting.
It added much to history
And to the ease of writing.

DIXON

Ticonderoga

NATION'S FIRST PENCIL

—now with gleaming metal tip!

Joseph Dixon Crucible Co., Dept. 52-J9, Jersey City 3, N. J.
Canadian Plant: Dixon Pencil Co., Ltd., Newmarket, Ont.

FOR THE ENJOYMENT OF LOVELIER, MORE RADIANT HAIR...MORE OFTEN

The Lady Sunbeam is so simple to use—just set the dial for any drying air temperature you want—hot, medium, warm or cool. Scientifically designed vinyl cap fits easily over your hair and concentrates drying air where hair is heaviest. Drying air comes from heat-control unit through durable, flexible hose. The Lady Sunbeam Hair Dryer eliminates the tiring arm raising and head turning necessary with ordinary hand held dryers—and annoying, uncomfortable hot air on neck and shoulders from professional type dryers. Cap has no electric wires. Only $24.95*

Only *Lady Sunbeam*
gives you all these advantages
● Greater convenience

Vitalis, 1951

Skol Tanning Lotion, 1956

Norcross Greeting Cards, 1957 ◀◀◀   Dixon Ticonderoga Pencils, 1950 ◀◀   Lady Sunbeam, 1957 ◀   Schick, 1957

153

RONALD REAGAN
starring in
"BEDTIME FOR BONZO"
a Universal-International
Picture
"JERIS rates cheers
for greaseless good grooming
and healthier, handsomer hair"
says Ronald Reagan

Women go for men with Handsome Hair!

For smooth, smart, suave, well groomed hair that women love and men admire, depend on Murray's famous hair preparations. Enjoy more popularity and romance, look better, feel more confident.

Keep your hair neat, handsome, natural looking all day long. Ask for Murray's today. On sale everywhere.

BILLY ECKSTINE
Famous singing Star of
"THE BIRD CAGE"
and featured on many MGM record hits.

JERIS gets my applause
for GLOSSY GOOD GROOMING,
and HEALTHIER, HANDSOMER HAIR,

says Billy Eckstine

NLY DANDRUFF-DESTROYING* JERIS HAS THIS ESH, CLEAN-SCENTED MASCULINE FRAGRANCE

all the hair tonics on the market, RIS and only JERIS brings you all these ir benefits: 1. *Glossy good grooming. Healthier, handsomer hair.* 3. *Scalp-mulation:* Daily JERIS massage helps omote healthy hair growth, relieves dry scalp, excessive falling hair. 4. *Destroys dandruff germs* on contact,* antiseptic action *instantly* removes ugly dandruff flakes. 5. *Exclusive masculine fragrance:* daily use of Jeris leaves hair clean-scented. Get Jeris today at drug counters — professional applications at barber shops everywhere. Jeris is not greasy to the touch, won't discolor coat collars, can't soil shirts, stain hats or upholstery. For greaseless good grooming insist on Jeris Hair Tonic.

JERIS KILLS DANDRUFF GERMS* ON CONTACT
*Pityrosporum ovale, which many authorities recognize as the cause of infectious dandruff is destroyed by Jeris Antiseptic Hair Tonic.

JERIS
ANTISEPTIC HAIR TONIC

Hair-Glo: A Medium weight dressing. Keeps hair looking natural.

Pomade: Makes it easy to control hair hard to manage.

Murray's HAIR-GLO
A Soft Dressing For All Types of Hair

MURRAY'S SUPERIOR HAIR DRESSING POMADE

Heads you win.. Hearts you win with Murray's.

Murray's
for well groomed hair

ACCEPT NO SUBSTITUTE

Murray's **SUPERIOR PRODUCTS COMPANY** Chicago 17, Illinois

© 1950

Five days of new freedom

Meds Tampons

YOUR FIRST PACKAGE FREE!

We know that once you try Meds®—the safer, softer tampon
and discover those five days of new freedom every month, you'll
a Meds tampon user ever after! Mail us the back panel from the fir
Meds box of 10 you buy, with your name and address. We'll return t
full price—39¢. Personal Products Corp., Dept. D-7, Milltown, N
(Offer expires Oct. 31, 1954.)

New Kotex napkins with the Kimlon center
protect better, protect longer.
Now Kotex adds the Kimlon center to increase absorbency, to keep stains from going through. With this inner fabric, the Kotex napkin stays even softer, holds its shape for perfect fit. Choose Kotex — the name you know best — in this smart new package.

KOTEX and KIMLON are trademarks of Kimberly-Clark Corp.

BROWNING AUTOMATIC-5

The Aristocrat of Automatic Shotguns

If years of satisfactory service under many and varied conditions will substantiate the excellence of a product, few of any type have so remarkably qualified as the Browning Automatic-5. Dependable, lasting, and effective performance in every kind of shotgunning the world over has justly earned it the name . . . Aristocrat of Automatic Shotguns.

It's built as you expect a Browning to be built—precision machined parts—personalized hand-fitting, hand-finishing, hand-engraving . . . and when you take command of this *all-round* performer, you will find its many distinctive features as pleasing as its construction is assuring.

12 or 16 gauge—Standard or Lightweight Models—from $127⁷⁵

5 shots as fast as you can pull the trigger—adapted to 3-shot capacity in seconds.

Convenient speed loading, 5 shells in 6 seconds. No other gun will load 5 shells as fast from shooting position through reload to shooting position.

Straight Sighting Plane—sharp and distinct from receiver to muzzle.

Exclusive Magazine Cutoff—Switch from one load to another in 2 seconds while retaining a full magazine—an unusual safety feature as well.

Shock Absorber—for comfortable shooting of any 2¾ inch shell.

See the Aristocrat . . . Be your own judge.

Write for Catalog

Write for new 28-page catalog showing all Browning guns in color, plus special chapters on shooting—practical information for gun enthusiasts. Address: Browning Arms Company, Department 62, St. Louis 3, Mo.

Prices subject to change without notice.

YOUR BROWNING DEALER

Browning Automatic Shotgun, 1957

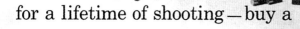

for a lifetime of shooting — buy a

PRICED FROM $104.95*

WINCHESTER
TRADEMARK

MODEL **12**

Good News! Only $10.95 down and up to 20 months to pay puts the superb Model 12 in your hands. See your local Winchester Time Payment Plan dealer for details.

WINCHESTER
FIREARMS
**TIME
PAYMENT
PLAN**

No shotgun made anywhere in the world can take it like a Model 12! Built of better materials, to a better design, by craftsmen to whom perfection is the only standard, a Winchester Model 12 is a treasured possession often handed from father to son. For 45 years the Model 12 has been the choice of sportsmen who know the best costs the least in the long run—make the 12 *your* choice, too.

action
pictures
prove

—that in less than 3/5 of a second a hunter can raise and fire a superbly balanced Model 12. Speed? You bet! The kind you must have for fast, fleet game.

**PRICES SUBJECT
TO CHANGE
WITHOUT NOTICE*

25 wear
adjustments

Tough Winchester Proof-Steel, machined to exact dimensions gives you years of extra use before any take-up is necessary. Then you can make a slight adjustment and get years more. *No Model 12 has ever used all the adjustment available!* Tough? And how!

WINCHESTER-WESTERN DIVISION · OLIN MATHIESON CHEMICAL CORPORATION · NEW HAVEN 4, CONN.

nchester Rifle, 1957

▶ *Crosley Electric Range, 1956*

You'll fall in love with the

BRIGHT NEW LOOK
IN HOME APPLIANCES!

NOW BROUGHT TO YOU BY

ADMIRAL

Behold the latest of the New Ideas—the "Fashion Front" on Admiral's new Refrigerator-Freezers! See how attractively you can decorate the door panel with wallpaper to match your kitchen! Or, there's a decorator kit of five different color panels optional with your new Dual-Temp. They're shiny, washable—pre-cut to fit—adhesive-backed so you can put them on and peel them off in a wink. Each change is as stimulating as a new hat! So give your kitchen the "Bright New Look"—with Admiral Appliances!

THE NEXT 5 PAGES TELL THE STORY OF *Admiral's* NEW IDEAS IN APPLIANCES...

No "pot-watching"!

MODEL J-408—$4.12 per week after small down payment*

Electric cooking is automatic! *Bake, boil, roast and grill without watching . . . even cook meals while you're away! New unit makes any pan automatic. Oven timer turns oven on and off by itself. Rotisserie barbecues automatically, too.*

MODEL J-408 *(shown above)* is G.E.'s finest range—embodies every G-E advance including: Famous G-E Keyboard Controls • *Two fully automatic ovens* • Master Oven with family-size rotisserie • Electric meat thermometer • Thrifty Companion Oven cooks dinner for six • New automatic surface unit, big removable griddle hold any temperature you set—*automatically!*

GENERAL ELECTRIC

Now...
cooks faster
than gas!

You get one of these new giant Speed-Cooking units on every G-E range

It's new ... it's test-proved! Every G-E range has one of the new Speed-Cooking units that's faster than gas. This 2600-watt unit was tested in G-E laboratories against the large burner of each of four leading gas stoves.

The G-E unit was faster in tests which included four pork chops in an aluminum skillet as illustrated. In addition, two cups, one quart and two quarts of water and a package of frozen peas were brought to a boil faster every time.

All G-E ranges also have big, extra-wide ovens, "Focused Heat" broilers, pushbuttons. Other de luxe models have automatic griddles, electric meat thermometers, automatic units, oven timers to "watch" meals, minute timers and other grand conveniences.

See all the Speed-Cooking ranges at your G-E dealer's . . . he's in the classified phone book.

General Electric Company, Appliance Park, Louisville 1, Kentucky.

Progress Is Our Most Important Product

GENERAL 🄶🄴 ELECTRIC

15.5 CU. FT. REFRIGERATOR-FREEZER: 34" WIDE, 65½" HIGH, 32 3/16" DEEP, MODEL DI15B

NEW! RCA WHIRLPOOL REFRIGERATOR-FREEZER
with exclusive Air Purifying System keeps food fresher...longer!

CUT FOOD SPOILAGE! Air Purifying System forces air through ultraviolet rays (1); retards growth of air-borne mold and bacteria! Cold, clean air recirculates (2) up the door (3).

END ICE TRAY TROUBLE! No more spilling! New ice tray filler* works with dial *inside* freezer; shuts itself off. New ice ejector zips out cubes, stores ice in server bin!

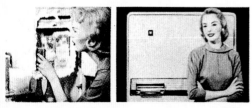

END DEFROSTING MESS! No more pans to empty, buttons to push! Automatic defrost system gets rid of frost and water in refrigerator section almost before it forms!

*optional at small extra cost.

Imagine! A full-size refrigerator up top with glide-out shelves, twin crispers, a big meat keeper *plus* a new self-filling ice water fountain*! A deep-set door with special food compartments, even shelves for ½-gal. bottles! Plus a 166-lb. freezer with glide-out basket, storage door, true "zero cold"! Backed by 50 years of refrigeration pioneering! Choice of colors, easy terms.

Whirlpool Corporation, St. Joseph, Michigan. (Use of trademarks ® and RCA authorized by trademark owner, Radio Corporation of America.

tpoint Refrigerators, 1953 ◄ *Whirlpool Refrigerators, 1957*   ► *General Electric Range, 1956*

New way to get big-range cooking in compact space

G-E Spacemaker has oven that holds meal for 24 . . .
4 Hi-Speed top units. Yet it takes up 16 inches less room

Do you need big-range cooking in small space? Or extra counters, storage room in a larger kitchen? This new G.E. is the answer. It has General Electric Speed-Cooking and most of the advantages of de luxe models, including color!

Huge floodlighted oven is so wide one shelf will hold 4 pies. 4 Calrod® pushbutton-controlled surface units give varied heats from barely warm to EXTRA-Hi-Speed. Drip pans and trays lift out to clean. There's a big storage drawer.

A fingertip touch and pushbuttons flick on just the heat you want. So easy even when your hands are full or wet. All surface units are fast-heating; one is General Electric's new giant Hi-Speed 2600-watt unit.

NEW! Oven-and-Minute Timer "watches" meals. Two simple clock settings and dinner cooks, heat goes off "by itself." For shorter baking or boiling jobs, a buzzer lets you know when cooking time's up.

"Charcoal Delicious" steaks, franks are easy with the General Electric "Focused Heat" broiler. It's quick, power-saving. Bake and broil units are fully enclosed. No old-fashioned open coils. Units slide out for easy oven cleaning.

Cooks Faster Than Gas!

It's new . . . it's test-proved! Every General Electric range has one of the new Speed-Cooking units that's faster than gas. This 2600-watt unit was tested in General Electric laboratories against the large burner of each of four leading gas stoves.

The General Electric unit was faster in tests which included four pork chops in an aluminum skillet. In addition, two cups, one quart and two quarts of water and a package of frozen peas were brought to a boil faster every time.

Easily Installed. Your G-E dealer can make arrangements for 220-volt wiring. Cost of range and required wiring can be financed with one low down payment and easy weekly terms.

Start your color-lovely G-E kitchen with this beautiful Speed-Cooking range in a Mix-or-Match color: turquoise green (as shown), canary yellow, cadet blue, petal pink, woodtone brown, satin white. A can of special, matching paint is all you need to "dress up" walls and cabinets.

See all the Speed-Cooking ranges at your G-E dealer's. He's in the classified phone book. General Electric Company, Appliance Park, Louisville 1, Kentucky.

Speed-Cooking ranges . . . so safe . . . so clean . . . so dependable

GENERAL ELECTRIC

YOU WANT THE WORLD'S FINEST AUTOMATIC WASHER

WORLD'S FIRST
AGITATOR-ACTION
AUTOMATIC

OF course you do. Then compare Blackstone's cleansing efficiency, beauty, structural excellence, and foolproof design with the others. See the Blackstone Automatic wash a big load of *really* soiled clothes. You'll know why Blackstone has received a *top bracket* rating in so many comparative tests by independent testing organizations. Ask your Blackstone dealer for a demonstration . . . he is listed in the Classified Telephone Directory.

WORLD'S ONLY
KITCHEN-MATCHED
AUTOMATIC LAUNDRY

THREE MATCHING UNITS
WASHER • DRYER • IRONER

WORLD'S ONLY
MECHANICALLY-CONTROLLED
AUTOMATIC

SEND FOR FREE BOOK
A factual, comparative analysis of current types of Automatic Washers.

THE
TRUTH
ABOUT
AUTOMATIC
WASHERS

BLACKSTONE CORPORATION,
Jamestown, New York

Please send a copy of your "TRUTH" booklet.

Name...

Address...

City.........................Zone........State..........

BLACKSTONE
WORLD'S OLDEST WASHER MANUFACTURER

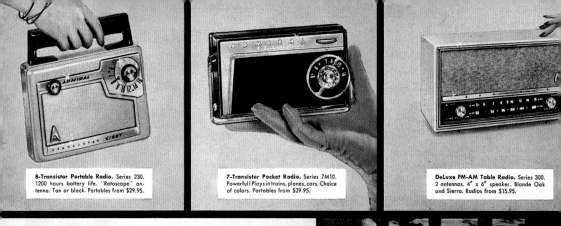

8-Transistor Portable Radio. Series 230. 1200 hours battery life. "Rotoscope" antenna. Tan or black. Portables from $29.95.

7-Transistor Pocket Radio. Series 7M10. Powerful! Plays in trains, planes, cars. Choice of colors. Portables from $29.95.

DeLuxe FM-AM Table Radio. Series 300. 2 antennas. 4" x 6" speaker. Blonde Oak and Sierra. Radios from $15.95.

FOR CHRISTMAS FROM

Admiral®

SON-R REMOTE CONTROL

Only remote control in the world that adjusts volume to 4 levels! No wires! No batteries! No stirring from your chair! New amazing SON-R also turns TV on-off, changes channels from anywhere in the room!

Look for this Christmas "Best Buy" tag when you shop. It's on specially selected Admiral products, so you can easily spot the Season's Best Gift Values.

High Fidelity FM-AM Radio-Phono. Series 410. 30-watt amplifier. 4 speakers. 4-speed changer. Sierra, Mahogany, or Blonde. As low as $4.15 a week.

Chairside High Fidelity Phono. Series 360. 4-speed changer. 3 speakers. Mahogany, Blonde Oak or Sierra veneers. As low as $1.50 a week.

Prices slightly higher some areas.

DeLuxe Table Radio. Series 270. Extra large 4" x 6" speaker. Completely finished back. White with Red, Turquoise, Gray. Table radios from $15.95.

High Fidelity Portable Phono. Series 340. 4-speed record changer. 8-watt amplifier. 2 speakers. Gold and Black or Tan and White. Portable phonos from $59.95.

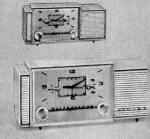

Super DeLuxe Clock Radio. Series 290. Wakes you, reminds you minutes later. Turns on appliances. White with Maroon, Gold, Green. Clock radios from $26.95.

Admiral's new "Thin as a Dime" styling has a glamorous new cabinet *barely over 16 inches deep.* It's the slimming magic of Admiral's new 110° picture tube. The old-fashioned bulge-in-the-back is gone, too! Your sleek new Admiral fits flush to the wall.

High Fidelity 21" TV, The Seton, Model CH21F54. Hi-Fi 4 speaker system. 8-watt amplifier. Plug in jack for record player. As low as $3.75 a week.

21 in. viewable area, 262 sq. in.

High Fidelity 21" TV, The Exeter, Model LHR21F33, PowerPack. 4 Hi-Fi speakers. Son-R available. As low as $4.20 a week.

BEST BUYS

Admiral

BEST BUY for CHRISTMAS

Slimline 21" Table TV, The Asbury, Model TR21E21. Two speakers with up-front sound. Matching base with "Lazy Susan" swivel. Charcoal, Mahogany, Blonde. As low as $2.70 a week. Available with Son-R remote control.

17 in. viewable area, 155 sq. in.

Slimline 17" Portable TV. Exclusive jolt-proof design. Thin cabinet only 13¾" deep. Power Tower antenna. Choice of colors. As low as $1.65 a week.

High Fidelity TV-Radio-Phono. The Canterbury, Model HFR21F42. Son-R Dual Remote Control. Mahogany, Blonde Oak, or Sierra veneer. As low as $5.40 a week.

Sit anywhere in the room

COLUMBIA STEREOPHONIC PHONOGRAPHS
PUT YOU IN THE CENTER OF SOUND

Here is the ultimate in listening—a new Columbia stereophonic phonograph. Turn it on and you're suddenly, dramatically in the Center of Sound—the place where music takes on a third dimension. Turn the remarkable Balanced Listening Control and you shift the Center of Sound wherever you want it. This Columbia engineering exclusive, available on many models, makes it possible for you to enjoy stereophonic sound in perfect proportion —not just in one spot, but *anywhere in the room!* Superb styling and cabinetry make every Columbia Stereo-Fidelity phonograph a truly matchless instrument for your home. Prices begin at only $124.90.

STEREO-FIDELITY PHONOGRAPHS BY COLUMBIA

NEWEST
GENERAL ELECTRIC
PORTABLE TV...

Terra Cotta & Ivory—Model 17T026
Bermuda Bronze—Model 17T025

56% BIGGER PICTURE

'Never before a TV so LIGHT...with a picture so BIG...so BRIGHT!

IT'S the new General Electric Portable TV with 56% bigger picture than previous designs. Yet, the weight of this newest G-E "take-around" marvel is still only *32 lbs.!* Mom, sis, even junior can carry it. Travels all around the house—all around the town—with the greatest of ease. Aluminized Picture Tube and dark safety window for "daylight power" picture—indoors and outdoors, even in fringe areas. And, big-screen G-E Portable TV is surprisingly low-priced...easily the BIGGEST bargain in TV pleasure you've ever seen.

With all the big *political* doings augmenting TV's most exciting sports events, spectaculars, who-dunnits and quiz shows, you'll be lots happier—so will your whole family—with an extra General Electric Portable TV in the house.

Now's the time to visit your General Electric TV dealer. See all that's excitingly new in G-E television advancements. And don't forget, G-E TV prices start at only $99.95. Now you can easily own two G-E TV for *less* than millions paid for one. General Electric Company, Television Receiver Department, Syracuse, New York.

Manufacturer's suggested retail prices include Federal Excise tax, increase courtesy on picture tube, 90 days on parts. UHF at small additional cost. Prices subject to change without notice.

See G.E. on TV: "Warner Bros. Presents" (ABC-TV) and "The 20th Century Fox Hour" (CBS-TV)

Striking "Sports-Car Styling". Sleek, colorful, only 32 lbs. light with advanced features galore. G-E Aluminized Picture Tube and aluminum cabinet. Adjustable rear leg for best viewing angle. Exclusive power cord compartment. Chrome-plated handle. Compact cabinet in Bermuda Bronze finish or two-tone Terra Cotta and Ivory.

Progress Is Our Most Important Product

GENERAL ELECTRIC

eneral Electric Television, 1956

G.E. DESIGNS NEW 32 lb. "PERSONAL" TV
Goes where you go...

SMART TWO-TONE CABINET in terra cotta and ivory. Built-in antenna. Chromium-coated handle. Model 14T009, above. Left, in gray and ivory, Model 14T008.

PATIO OR PICNIC—you need never be without your G-E TV! Just bring it along. Life's more fun with Portable TV!

ROOM TO ROOM television is easy with G-E Personal TV. So light or so small you can carry it wherever it's needed most.

FOR THE KITCHEN, by lightest household chores...(or catch shows you like to see, while hubby watches the football games!

TOPS FOR TRIPS! Your new G-E Portable TV tucks easily into luggage compartment. Light enough to carry anywhere!

FOR TAKE-IT-WITH-YOU USE—from $99.95
indoors...outdoors...all around the house!

TURNS ON-OFF AUTOMATICALLY. Clock-TV Model 14T010, house and ivory. 2-way interference protection. Recessed handle beneath clock. Most useful TV ever.

ONLY $99.95. Ideal for bedrooms, den, kitchen, wherever an extra television set is needed. Makes a grand gift, too. Model 14T007 in cordovan finish.

Put an end to TV traffic jams...family squabbles over which show to see! Get G.E.'s new 32-lb. TV—the ideal roving extra set. Never before—TV so useful, so light! Even Sis can carry it, from room to room, anywhere.

Just plug it in. You'll be amazed at the bright, clear picture. Has built-in antenna. Choice of striking two-tone color combinations with new car look and verve. So low in price, you'll want two of 'em! P.S.—makes a wonderful gift!

☆ ☆ ☆ ☆

For top value in big-picture TV, look into G.E.'s 21 and 24-inch models. You'll see more features for less money than ever before. You'll enjoy G.E.'s "Daylight Power". It makes the picture so bright, you can watch with shades up, lights on! See your General Electric Dealer. Learn how you can buy your G-E set for less than millions paid for only one! General Electric Company, Radio & Television Department, Syracuse, New York.

Prices include Federal Excise tax, one-year warranty on picture tube, 90 days on parts. Prices subject to change without notice.

See G.E. on TV: "Warner Bros. Presents" (ABC-TV) and "The 20th Century Fox Hour" (CBS-TV)

NEW G-E CLOCK-TV console—for folks who like to watch the late shows. Turns itself off automatically after you fall asleep. Wakes you in the A.M. Reminds you of favorite programs. 21-inch. Model 21C115.

NEW G-E 24-INCH TV—for biggest, brightest, clearest picture in the whole neighborhood! Big performance, too, with G-E Daylight Power...famous G-E Aluminized Tube...dark safety glass. Model 24C181.

Progress Is Our Most Important Product

GENERAL ELECTRIC

umbia Stereophonic Phonographs, 1958 ◀   *General Electric Television, 1955*   ▶ *Magnavox Television, 1951*

Look! Portable TV from $129.95
It's a wonderful Christmas

Easy to see why Santa delivers more RCA Victor TV than any other kind. No other TV offers so many fine features or such a choice of models— 47 of them, completely new inside and out.

New lean, clean and mirror-sharp black-and-white TV. Dramatically slender and clean of line, it fits beautifully where other TV couldn't go at all. Cabinets are up to 9½ inches slimmer! And look at the *variety:* trim table models, TV that rolls, swivels and even fits *in corners.*

Listen to it! That's Balanced Fidelity Sound— the finest! You also get the newest tuning fea-

tures and "One-Touch" on-off control.
New "Flight-Line" Portables. Breezy, easy-going TV to take along, in every popular size. Popular prices, too. Your ideal second set.

Most important, every model gives you RCA Victor's new "Mirror-Sharp" picture for the sharpest, clearest contrasts in TV!
New "Living Color" TV, including the superb new Mark Series. The happiest surprise a Santa could put under any tree, the gift of color! It's *performance-proved*—backed by service records from tens of thousands of homes. The colors

come in bright, natural, with realism
near startling. Tuning is a snap. The
holds sure and steady. And you get grea
programs every day *plus* all the bla
white shows.

Contact your favorite Santa or TV d
and ask for RCA Victor TV *soon*—you'
sure of a wonderful Christmas.

rner TV-lowboys-Living Color!
RCA Victor land!

GIVE "THE GIFT THAT KEEPS ON GIVING"

RCA VICTOR
RADIO CORPORATION OF AMERICA

LISTENING IN DEPTH

A NEW EXPERIENCE IN "360" HIGH-FIDELITY EXCLUSIVE WITH COLUMBIA

First, Columbia gave you the modern long-playing record. Then, famous "360" sound, which brought high fidelity into your living room. Now, for this Christmas, Columbia research brings you a new adventure in sound. Directed Electromotive Power (D.E.P.*) introduces the miracle of the sealed sound chamber for tonal balance throughout the *entire* listening range. By exploring the whole universe of human hearing, both subconscious and

conscious, Columbia now makes it possible for you and your famil perience the excitement of "Listening in Depth."

There are more than thirty-five 1958 Columbia Phonographs which the new characteristics of "360" sound . . . portables, consoles, c tions, in a wide and attractive price range. As a treasured gift at Ch nothing can match the pleasure of a high-fidelity Columbia Phor

THE GREATEST NAME IN SOUND . . . *enjoy the Sound of Genius on Columbia Records . . . protect your valuable records with Columbia Acc*

from \$29.95 to \$1,995 . . . COLUMBIA PHONOGRAPI

® "Columbia" "360" ⚡ Marcas Reg.

Fabulous *FEDERAL* COOKWARE!

Fabulous *PINK*

Fabulous PRICES

99¢

(2 QT. SAUCEPAN WITH COVER)

ADVERTISED IN **LIFE**

FEDERAL VOGUE ENAMELED WARE TITANIUM ADDED FOR EXTRA LIFE
FEDERAL ENAMELING & STAMPING CO. PITTSBURGH U.S.A.

Easy-to-clean PORCELAIN ENAMELED WARE!

Now, have the year's most fashionable cookware color — PINK — and have it at low prices you thought were *out* of fashion! Now, cook, serve, store in the same pot — yet pay *less* than you ever believed possible. No other cookware is so easy-to-clean *completely* — so sanitary. Yesterday's flavors never stay for today; even your most delicate sauces will be cooked to perfection. The price will never be better . . . the color is *right* — and *permanent*. See Federal Vogue PINK enameled ware today!

AT YOUR FAVORITE HOUSEWARES COUNTER

FEDERAL VOGUE ENAMELED WARE *Titanium added for extra life*

FEDERAL ENAMELING AND STAMPING CO.

Windsor shape Open Sauce Pans. Set of three, ⅝, 1, 1½ qts....1.49

Pudding Pan with rolled rim. 1¾ qt. size...49c, 3½ qt....59c

Percolator with aluminum inset. Generous 8 cup size.........1.69

Flavor-Saver Covered Pots. Handy 3⅞ qt. size...1.49, 5⅜ qt....1.79

2 qt. Tea Kettle (wood grip)...1.49 Family-style 5 qt. size.........1.98

8" Fry Pan. Easy to clean and so attractive to hang on wall.....99c

Oval Dish Pan, 9¼ qt. size...1.39 Round, 8¾ qt. 1.19 — 11½ qt. 1.39.

Combination Cooker. You can use it five different ways. 2 qt......1.89

Prices may vary slightly according to location

A Kitchen-Size
DIXIE CUP Dispenser
ends between-meal clutter!

- No more piled-up counters and sinks!
- No more between-meal dishwashing!
- No more glasses to be dried and put away!
- No more broken glasses!
- Handy for the whole family...the year 'round!
- For fruit juices! Milk! Soft drinks!
- Ideal for outdoors during hot summer months!

Look for the big economy size... the thrifty way to buy Dixie Cups for everyday home use

Dixie is a registered trade mark of the Dixie Cup Company

! Dixie Cups Do So Much...Cost So Little !

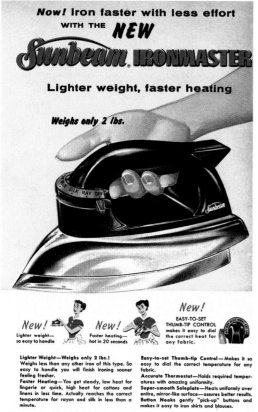

Sunbeam Ironmaster

Sunbeam Mixmaster

▶ Sunbeam Mixmaster, 19

Royal Chi-net Paper Plates, 1956

Pyrex, 1954

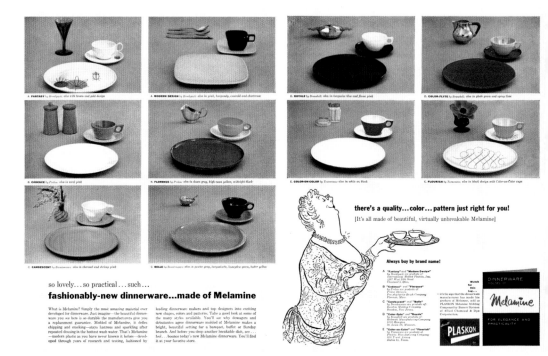

Melamine Dinnerware, 1956

▶ *American Cynamid Company, 19*

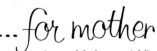

...for mother
... because she's always wanted dinnerware
that's beautiful and guaranteed
break-resistant, too!

for the bride...
... because Melmac dinnerware is so smart,
so colorful, so carefree to use
she'll enjoy it happily ever after!

...for yourself
... because you want dinnerware that sets
lovely tables for your important dinners
and brightens up your everyday meals, too!

MELMAC®
dinnerware

Melmac quality melamine dinnerware
is guaranteed by its molders for a full year
against breaking, cracking and chipping.

Melmac is quality molded dinnerware
but not all molded dinnerware is Melmac.

Melmac is found in leading stores
under individual molder's brand names.

Look for the Melmac tag.

CYANAMID

MELMAC® quality melamine dinnerware

MELMAC is the registered trade-mark of American Cyanamid
Company, New York 20, N. Y., supplier of molding compounds to manufacturers of quality melamine dinnerware.

Melmac Dinnerware, 1956

▶ *Melmac Dinnerware, 1953* ▶ ▶ *The Home Insurance Company, 1*

another adventure of the *Ozzie Nelsons...*

"Hey, Big Noise—how's this for a painting? I'm an artist!!"

["This kid's got to go!"] "Look, Genius—mine's been done for half an hour. C'mon, let's show Mom and Pop."

they paint original *Picture Craft* oil paintings

"Yes... families everywhere are painting original *Picture Craft!"*

Just like the Ozzie Nelsons ... you, too, will prefer original Picture Craft. An exclusive process enables you to re-create a true work of art. It's fun, relaxing, you need no experience—and it's GUARANTEED!

• • • •

The leader for over 15 years, original Picture Craft is the *only* "paint-by-numbers" kit that gives you: true pre-mixed artist's colors ... a specially treated artist's canvas ... and an exclusive 4-in-1 brush designed by Picture Craft. It all adds up to the ideal hobby for you ... the perfect gift for a friend.

Guaranteed by Good Housekeeping bears this seal

Original Picture Craft bears this seal

Kit includes:
• NUMBERED ARTIST'S CANVAS (16" x 12")
• PRE-MIXED OIL COLORS
• SPECIAL ARTIST'S BRUSH
• SIMPLE PAINTING INSTRUCTIONS

CHOOSE FROM 35 BEAUTIFUL SUBJECTS

ONLY $2.95 COMPLETE KIT

Picture Craft Frames at Slight Extra Cost

At better Department • Art • Hobby • Stationery • Camera and Paint Stores ... or write to:

PAINT A BEAUTIFUL PICTURE IN OILS
Picture Craft
NO EXPERIENCE • NO LESSONS • NO MIXING

790 N. WATER STREET • DECATUR, ILL.

Enjoy "The Adventures of Ozzie & Harriet" on radio and TV each week on ABC sponsored by Hotpoint and Listerine.

Jackets & Jeans by Blue Ridge Mfg. Co. Jackets $2.79, Jeans $2.79

Wrist Watches (Roy Rogers & Dale Evans) by Bradley Time Corp. $4.95 plus F.T. Alarm Clock (not illustrated) $3.95 plus F.T.

Roy Rogers Hats by Sackman Bros. Ass'd colors $1.98

Frontier Shirts by Rob Roy Long sleeve $2.95, Short $1.95

Boots & Felt Slippers by S. Goldberg & Co., Inc. All styles $1.99

Boots & Tex-Tans by Tex Tan of Yoakum Boots $7.95 up, Tex-Tans $3.79

Roy Rogers "Shootin' Irons" by Kilgore (Model left) ....$1.00 (Model right) 79c

Roy Rogers Lunch Kit by The American Thermos Bottle Co. Complete with ½ pint bottle $2.89

A Summer of Fun with ROY ROGERS

Guaranteed Products

Whenever you get the youngster in your life something "just like Roy's," you can be sure you're getting value for your money. Roy Rogers' "Pledge To Parents" assures you that a leading manufacturer has made a quality product to satisfy *you* as well as your youngster. You can buy Roy Rogers branded merchandise with confidence.

ROY ROGERS GUN & HOLSTER SE
by Classy Products
Young cowhands "go" for these gen holsters of hand-worked quality lea Rust-proof nickel studs, adjustable s and Western Buckle.
Upper, deluxe model ....$
Lower, Two-gun, Deputy style ....
Other models from $1.98 to $10.5

ROY ROGERS T-SHIRTS & SWEAT SHIRTS
by Norwich Mills Inc.
Roy and Trigger design on fine qu cotton, with reinforced seams and i lock collars. In White, Blue or G Guaranteed to take many washings. Short sleeve T-Shirt ....
Long sleeve Sweat Shirt ....$

ROY ROGERS PLEDGE TO PARENTS

This item of merchandise, bearing my name, has been tested in one of the nation's largest testing bureaus and, in our judgment, equals in quality any merchandise selling in the same price range. You pay no premium for my name. Rather, it is your assurance that this item is an authentic value.

Roy Rogers

Shop your local retailer. He has these items or can get them for you

ROY ROGERS 1418 North Highland Avenue

ENTERPRIS Hollywood 28, Califo

Insurance By North America, 1957 ◀ *Picture Craft, 1955*

Roy Rogers Enterprises, 1954

HOPALONG CASSIDY

ACME COWBOY BOOTS

ACME
HOPALONG

NEW OFFICIAL DESIGN

COMMENDED BY THE CONSUMER SERVICE BUREAU OF **PARENTS'** MAGAZINE ADVERTISED IN...

For boys and girls, priced according to size . . .

6.95 to 12.95

Here's your pal . . . HOPALONG CASSIDY . . .
and his <u>brand</u> <u>new</u> cowboy boots!

That's right, boys and girls! . . . these handsome new boots are Hoppy's very own! You'll be proud to own them, and you'll really get a lot of fun wearing them!

You'll enjoy their beauty and comfort for a long time, because they are made by the most expert craftmen at Acme, the world's largest makers of cowboy boots! Get your pair right away!

Your Acme dealer has a colorful assortment of these brand new Hopalong Cassidy cowboy boots! See them as soon as you can!

"Tested in the stirrup . . . where it really counts"

ACME BOOT COMPANY, CLARKSVILLE, TENNESSEE

World's largest makers of cowboy boots

opalong Cassidy Boots, 1951

Celanese Corporation of America, 1950 ◄   Mouseketeer Hat, 1955

Luxury Liner

ROADMASTER

Merry Xmas

What dreams are made o

A bright, shiny Roadmaster Christmas! The slick-riding bike
everything a boy and girl want... electric horn, brake-operated s
bumpers and Searchbeam headlight. A dream co

Just what mom and dad want, too...
the extra strength and safety of
Roadmaster's 100% electronically welded frame.
Write for our free catalog, then see your dealer.

CLEVELAND WELDING CO., W. 117th St. and Berea Rd., Cleveland, Ohio. Subsidiary of AMERICAN MACHINE & FOUNDRY COMPANY,

It's Thrifty...it's Smart and so _Easy_ to ride!

HARLEY-DAVIDSON 125
POWER RIDING FOR EVERYONE!

ENJOYABLE PERSONAL TRANSPORTATION

AT LOW COST
FOR EVERYBODY

If you have never ridden a Harley-Davidson 125, you have a big, pleasant surprise coming! Lightweight and low center of gravity make balancing almost automatic. Control is simple and sure. One lesson and you'll be able to go anywhere quickly, dependably and at amazingly _low cost!_ 90 miles and more per gallon, practically no upkeep, no parking fees. Good looking, too, streamlined, colorful. Smooth, quiet performance with such advanced automotive features as brakes on both wheels, 3-speed transmission, drop-forged steering head, oversize tires, easy-chair saddle, brilliant night lighting. Thousands in use by men, women, boys, girls, for work, business, school, errands, outings. You owe it to yourself to _try_ it. "A penny saved is a penny earned" and think of the _fun_ you can have! Low down payment, easy terms. Phone or see your Harley-Davidson dealer for a FREE ride.

MAIL THE COUPON NOW!

HARLEY-DAVIDSON MOTOR CO., Dept. C, Milwaukee 1, Wisconsin
Send colorful folder and full information about the low-cost Harley-Davidson 125.

Name.....................................

Address.................................

City....................................State.................

DEALERS: Valuable franchises available for the full line of famous Big Twins and the 125 model. Your opportunity to line up with the greatest name in motorcycles. Write or wire for information today.

HARLEY-DAVIDSON 125
POWER RIDING FOR EVERYONE!

Built especially for YOU!

YOUNG or old, this is _your_ two-wheeler! So easy to ride, you learn in one lesson! So economical, you get 90 miles and more per gallon. So convenient and dependable, you'll want to ride it everywhere . . . to factory, office, store, school, sports events, outings. Frees you from crowded buses and trolleys. Saves your car. Ends parking problems and traffic troubles. Smartly modern, streamlined, and colorful. Remarkably comfortable with "easy chair" saddle, big tires. Smooth, quiet performance. Built for safety with brakes on both wheels, 3-speed transmission, brilliant lighting. And so easy on your pocketbook! Small down payment and it's yours. Then pay as you ride as you save! Phone or see your dealer today!

MAIL THE COUPON NOW!

HARLEY-DAVIDSON MOTOR CO., Dept. C-2, Milwaukee 1, Wisconsin
Send colorful folder and full information about the NEW, low-cost, economical-to-operate Harley-Davidson 125.

Name.....................................

Address.................................

City....................................State.................

DEALERS: Valuable franchises available for the full line of famous Big Twins and 125 Model. Write today.

admaster Bicycle, 1952 ◄ _Harley-Davidson, 1950_

Harley-Davidson, 1950

M552
75mm RADAR AA
SKYSWEEPER

When this kit is com
only description
"Jewel-Like." Ever
this automatic rada
is faithfully repro
134 precision parts
of the intricate, fu
tures of the prot
plete model has 3
operating assembli
gun barrel that actu
strates recoil actio
contains shells w
loaded or unloade
ting munition retai
plete with 5 life-like
bers consisting of
Radar Operator, Co
ator, Loader and A
Authentic decals in

Packed: 1 dozen to
Weight: 10 lbs.

M553
280mm Gun
ATOMIC
CANNON

It takes 279 parts to make up this detailed model of the Army's largest mobile artillery piece and the specially designed front and rear trucks that transport it. (Actually 3 kits in 1.) Super-detailed throughout, the finished model is fully operative...it does everything but fire! Cannon is detachable from trucks and elevates by hand wheel and gear train. Gun barrel telescopes 6" from travelling position to firing position. Each truck has six free rolling wheels. Kit complete with 7 lifelike crew members consisting of Commander, 2 drivers, 2 munition haulers with cart and shells, 2 gunners. Authentic decals included.

Packed: 1/3
Weight: App

enting...
models!

M551
Self Propelled 8 inch
HOWITZER

Packed: 1 dozen to carton
Weight: Approx 18 lbs.

138 parts that make up the most authentically detailed kit ever offered in any price range. When assembled, the builder has a model that truly captures all the power and excitement of this famous Army weapon. Renwal's engineering insures positive assembly and exclusive "NO SHOW" cementing design eliminates all messy stains. Assembled model has 37 authentic operating parts that include all doors, hatches, gun, turret, engine, tread and wheels. Detailed interior is visible through operating doors. Kit comes complete with 6 lifelike crew members consisting of Commander, Driver, Gunner, Loader, Radio Operator and Technician. Authentic Decals included.

U.S. ARMY ★ 551

Big Shot

U.S. ARMY ★ M553

LITTLE RED SCHOOLHOUSE

Regulation-Size Building Bricks

Sturdy, colorful chest comes filled with 24 rugged regulation-size fibre building bricks all assembled.

Illustrations for basic uses of Bricks and play school-house on inside cover for effective store display.

Take out Bricks and Chest very simply becomes attractive play school-house which can be used in the building scheme.

SLINKY®

ALL NEW and TIMELY!

SLINKY SATELLITE BEANIE

FOR BOYS AND GIRLS!
UNBREAKABLE PLASTIC

Kids will demand them. Satellite bobs back and forth as head moves Slinky spring motion. Complete with strap and constellation headband decoration.

$1.29   **CATALOG NO. 325**

1 doz. per carton. Weight 7 lbs.

NEW

NEW

SLINKY POPUP

Push down on spring—then wait for him to blow his top. Fun for *adults and children*. Packed for counter or rack.

69c   **Catalog No. 450**

2 doz. per carton
Weight 4 lbs.

NEW

SLINKY SPINNER

Makes its own orbit! A *different* action. Top whirls and jumps around. Packed for counter or rack.

79c   **Catalog No. 175**

2 doz. per carton. Weight 5 lbs.
Minimum prepaid weight 200 lbs.

Here's proof that luxuries needn't be expensive!

Argus C-3—*only* **$66.50** *complete with case and flash*

No other 35mm camera in all the world offers you so many luxury features for the money! The Argus C-3 has a color-corrected f:3.5 Cintar lens; gear-controlled shutter with speeds up to 1/300 second; easy-to-use Color-matic settings; lens-coupled rangefinder; built-in flash synchronization—the flashgun plugs right into the camera. And the C-3 is the only American-made camera that offers you a selection of interchangeable lenses that make it versatile as cameras costing hundreds of dollars more!

See the amazing Argus C-3 at your dealer's today.

These two interchangeable lenses make the C-3 perform like cameras costing hundreds of dollars more

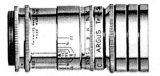

Argus C-3 Telephoto Lens. It cuts distances in half—lets you take candid closeups from twice as far away as with a regular lens. This 100mm f:4.5 lens automatically couples to the rangefinder. The smooth, helical action makes focusing just as easy as with the regular lens. Only $49.50. (Leather case extra.)

Argus C-3 Wide-Angle Lens: This lens gives you a broader, taller field of view—87% more picture area—than with the standard lens. This 35mm f:4.5 lens easily interchanges with the Cintar lens and is coupled to the rangefinder for sure, easy focusing. Only $49.50. (Leather case extra.)

Easy to use...Easy to own...That's Argus!
Most dealers offer convenient credit terms

Color photographs to fight crime!

Law enforcement officers now have a valuable new tool in ANSCO Color Printon . . . low cost color photographs that give a realistic record of the scene of a crime or accident. Details in full color show unmistakable evidence, leave less ground for doubt or evasion, confirm and support witnesses' reports. ANSCO Printon will save time in police investigations and court procedure . . . save money for litigants and taxpayers.

Printon will also make it possible for local police departments to have color photographs of criminals of record, for easier, more positive identification.

Transparencies taken with ordinary cameras on ANSCO color film, give Printon prints in full color . . . can be bought for as little as $3.00 for a large 8 x 10 inch print—*or can be developed in your own darkroom!*

ANSCO research in photography improves film, cameras, processes . . . makes picture taking and printing easier for everybody, assures better pictures at lower cost. Five hundred factory tests of ANSCO film are your guaranty of more satisfactory pictures.

MAKING cameras and photographic supplies since 1842, and today a Division of General Aniline & Film, ANSCO is the second largest U. S. producer of film, photographic papers and cameras . . . Another GAF Division at Johnson City, N. Y. makes Ozalid®, the most efficient facsimile copying machine, and sensitized materials . . . With large plants at Rensselaer, N. Y. and Grasselli, N. J., General Aniline is this country's largest manufacturer of quality dyestuffs and a large supplier of industrial chemicals *(sold through General Dyestuff Corporation)* . . .

General Aniline provides good jobs for more than 7,500 people . . . spends more than $35 million a year for wages and salaries, $5 million in research, $12 million in taxes. It's a good company to work for or with, and worth watching.

General Aniline & Film Corporation
*From Research to Reality...*230 Park Ave., New York 17, N. Y.

◄ *Argus, 1956   General Aniline & Film Corporation, 1952*

Enter-
tainment
210

RRYL F. ZANUCK
presents

GREGORY PECK

JENNIFER JONES
in 20th Century-Fox's

FREDRIC MARCH

"The Man in the Gray Flannel Suit"

The outstanding
best-seller
now an
outstanding
motion picture...
with the year's
outstanding
cast!

co-starring

marisa pavan
lee j. cobb
ann harding
keenan wynn
gene lockhart

GREGORY PECK
as Tom Rath

JENNIFER JONES
as Betsy Rath

FREDRIC MARCH
as Hopkins

MARISA PAVAN
as Maria

LEE J. COBB
as Judge Bernstein

ced by
RRYL F. ZANUCK
n for the Screen and
ed by
NNALLY JOHNSON

COLOR by DE LUXE CinemaScopE®

From the novel by SLOAN WILSON

One of the spectacular thrills: the searing siege of Greek Fire! An army of beautiful women . . . against an army of violent men!

HOWARD HUGHES presents

SON OF SINBAD

starring

DALE ROBERTSON · SALLY FORREST

LILI ST. CYR · VINCENT PRICE · co-starring MARI BLANCHARD

Directed by TED TETZLAFF · Written by AUBREY WISBERG
and JACK POLLEXFEN · Produced by ROBERT SPARKS

THE NEW ANAMORPHIC PROCESS
SUPERSCOPE
ON THE GIANT WIDE SCREEN

color by
TECHNICOLOR

Exotic, seductive, revealing dances . . . such as you have never seen before!

Son Of Sinbad, 1950

HOWARD HUGHES presents
JANE RUSSELL
IN UNDERWATER!

ENTER that new, thrilling Underwater World...with Jane Russell as you've never seen her before!

It took 3 years to make...cost $3,000,000!

THE NEW ANAMORPHIC PROCESS
SUPERSCOPE
ON THE GIANT WIDE SCREEN
color by TECHNICOLOR

co-starring
GILBERT ROLAND · RICHARD EGAN · LORI NELSON · Directed by JOHN STURGES · Screenplay by WALTER NEWMAN · Produced by HARRY TATELMAN

derwater, 1955

▶ Trapeze, 1956

THE WONDER SH

It Happens There,
In Mid-Air...
In All Its Fire, Flesh And Fury!

TRA

W OF THE WORLD!

HECHT AND LANCASTER present

BURT
LANCASTER

TONY
CURTIS

GINA LOLLOBRIGIDA

EZE

IN
CINEMASCOPE
COLOR by De Luxe

CIRCUS

d by   Screen play by   Adaptation by   Released thru

MES HILL · JAMES R. WEBB · LIAM O'BRIEN · A SUSAN PRODUCTIONS INC. Picture · UNITED ARTISTS

All the sultry drama of Tennessee Williams' Pulitzer Prize Play is now on the s

M·G·M
presents

Cat
on a Hot
Tin Roof

This
is
Maggie
the
Cat...

starring

ELIZABETH TAYLOR
PAUL NEWMAN
BURL IVES

JACK CARSON · JUDITH ANDERSON

Screen Play by RICHARD BROOKS and JAMES POE · Based on the Play "CAT ON A HOT TIN ROOF" by TENNESSEE WILL

in METROCOLOR · AN AVON PRODUCTION · Directed by RICHARD BROOKS · Produced by LAWRENCE WEINGARTE

Cat on a Hot Tin Roof, 1958   I Married A Communist, 1950

Fashion
& Beauty
220

IT'S A BLOUSE...IT'S A SLIP...ALL IN ONE!

Blue Swan Slipmates

SCHOOL · SPORTS

HOME · WORK

$2.98

SIZES 32 (dress 9/10) to 40 (dress 17/18)
Also TEEN SIZES for ages 10-12-14

- **ECONOMICAL** . . . *Serves a Double Purpose!*
- **FASHIONABLE** . . . *Styled For Wear Almost Everywhere!*
- **NEAT** . . . *The Blouse Can't Slip Out!*
- **SMOOTH-FITTING** . . . *Cut From Exacting Slip Patterns!*
- **PRACTICAL** . . . *As Easy To Wash As a Regular Slip!*

Just slip into Slipmates — step into a skirt and you're smartly dressed! Wonderful for wear with a suit too! The blouse top is styled with the popular "bat" sleeves in soft interlock combed cotton jersey with a smart heather effect. Permanently attached is a runproof tricot rayon half slip that beautifully molds to your figure. A clever new idea — at an unbelievably low price.

Hurry to your favorite store for your Slipmates today!

Blouse tops in a choice of lovely heather tones.

GOLDEN ERA YELLOW · DRAMATIC RED · FLIGHT BLUE · GLAMOUR PINK
DYNAMIC GREEN · AUTUMN RUST · FROSTY WHITE

JUST ADD A SK

CREATORS OF
Suspants and M

Available at Knit Lingerie Departments and Specialty Shops or write
BLUE SWAN MILLS, DIV. OF McKAY PRODUCTS CORP., 350 FIFTH AVE., N.Y.

EXTRA ★

THE DAILY TRIBUNE

FINAL MARKETS
SPECIAL
SPORTS REVIEW

NATION'S HEADLINE DAILY

PAGE 1

EAUTY DISAPPEARS !
YSTERY FIGURE HIDES

Outposts of Atomic Age
Now Encircle Globe

Shown:
Etude* Minor Strapless
with
concealed bust pads...
the foam rubber

the genius of Peter Pan shapes a beautiful future!

PETER PAN

There's a more exciting summer in store for you! Choose the Peter Pan strapless bra made to make you look your loveliest in all your bare-shoulder fashions:

FREEDOM RING† *(left)*, a new revolutionary *wired* bra that brings you peace of mind—unique spring action takes all irritating pressure off sensitive areas. Comes with Hidden Treasure or Inner Circle cup.

INNER CIRCLE * *(center)*, for the average or full-average bust. The exclusive Dura-form cup guarantees uplift that *keeps up* for the long life of the bra.

HIDDEN TREASURE * *(right)*, the most famous bra in the world, for the small bust or in-between size. The patented Magicup adds fullness *confidentially*, without pads or puffs.

PETER PAN FOUNDATIONS, INC.

FIFTH AVENUE, NEW YORK

MERRY-GO-ROUND OF CANADA, MONTREAL, QUEBEC

* REG. U. S. PAT. OFF. † PATS.

◄◄◄ *American Optical, 1959*   ◄◄ *Slipmates, 1950*   ◄ *Maidenform, 1954*   *Peter Pan Foundations, Inc., 1954*   ► *Sarong Girdles, 1*

Style 124, high-waisted Sarong of light nylon power net and embroidered nylon marquisette. White, black or pink. Sizes 25 to 34. $13.50. Other styles from $7.95.

she's wearing a **sarong**®

the criss-cross girdle that walks and won't ride up

Sarong is completely different from any other girdle—and you'll feel the difference immediately!
There is nothing like a Sarong to fashion your figure with new shapeliness, to make comfort
your personal and permanent possession. Sarong is so wonderfully different!
Its patented, hidden construction lifts and flattens your tummy youthfully. Its exclusive
patented criss-cross feature lets you walk, stand and sit with day-long comfort.
From the moment you slip it on—you'll see and feel your figure improve.
Why not plan to have a Sarong fitted to your figure.

Free! Sarong's new booklet "Facts About Figures".
Write Sarong, Inc., Department MC-1, 200 Madison Avenue, New York 16, N.Y.

registered trademark
nc. for its girdles."

sarong
the patented girdle

with the criss-cross front

a feast for the eyes!

What more could a man ask for! Just one touch of new, soft, smooth,
Vanuana Sport Shirts and you'll be humming "Sweet Leilani" all
season long. As luxurious and rich-looking as a tropical paradise . . . as
cool and exciting as a night in Waikiki. Sixteen bright, solid, South Sea
colors that dance before your eyes. Short sleeves. **$3.65** or long sleeves. **$4.50.**

Phillips-Jones Corp., N. Y. 1, N. Y., Makers of Van Heusen Shirts • Sport Shirts • Ties • Pajamas • Handkerchiefs • Collars

Van Heusen
REG T. M.

Vanuana sport shirts

Fashion Academy Award

McGregor, 1959

◄◄ Be-Bop Glasses, 1950   ◄◄ Revlon, 1957   ◄ Van Heusen, 1951   Dan River, 1955

...angler, 1956

Dickies, 1955

...tes Fabrics, 1952 ◄ *Dan River, 1957*

Smartly Tailored
for Smart Relaxing

Look as good as you feel in your "easy-time" clothes!

These distinguished new Arrow Sports Shirts were made to give you casual comfort with the smartest style this side of Bikini. Tailored of a premium all-rayon fabric that's color-fast and WASHABLE, these eye-catching prints come in more color combinations than you ever imagined! Short sleeves, $5. Some with long sleeves, $5.95. Cluett, Peabody & Co., Inc.

Arrow Caribbean Prints

Another smartly styled ARROW SPORTS SHIRT

Arrow, 1953

With a Flair
for casual
smartness

Want comfort? Want good looks, too? Get yourself an Arrow Dude Ranch sport shirt. This collection includes beautifully tailored neat checks and plaids. It features the regular-length sports shirt collar, or new short points. (The collars on all Arrow sports shirts have the new *Arafold* construction that makes them look, fit, feel better.) Fabrics are colorfast, "Sanforized" cottons. $3.95. Why not pick out a few now. Cluett, Peabody & Co., Inc.

Arrow dude ranch

Another smartly styled ARROW SPORTS SHIRT

Arrow, 1953

Put some romance
in your "loof life"!

ARROW
Bali Cay

Whether you're taking a cruise to the Caribbean or just a week-end jaunt to the beach, do it with a splash! Add some color to the landscape; pick up an armful of Arrow Bali Cays!

These beauties are as colorful as a coral reef ... and just as washable! They come in big, splashy patterns and small, neat designs in both cotton and rayon fabrics. In short or long sleeves. And all have the amazing Arafold Collar. Prices about $4.50 and up (Subject to government regulation.) See Bali Cay at your Arrow dealer's now!

Cluett, Peabody & Co., Inc., Arrow Shirts • Sports Shirts • Ties • Handkerchiefs • Underwear

Arrow, 1952

Turning leaves splash the Autumn scene with spectacular hues...inspire new shirts with subtle stripes, lavish plaids in the

COLORS OF INDIAN SUMMER

...for the look of the leader

McGregor captures the brilliant changing landscapes of Fall —reaps a harvest of warm, glowing color—in a magnificent new shirt collection of luxurious, washable cotton by Dan River. (left) Kernel III—button-down, back-button, back-pleat Ivy Leaguer. $6.95. (right) Kernel II—new soft roll collar. Fine plaid on distinctive stripes. $6.95. (center) Kernel VI—woven-cotton pullover with fashion-knit collar. $6.95.

Lamb Fleece Cru Sweaters in the colors of Indian Summer. 75% luxurious lambswool for warmth without weight—25% rugged Orlon for washability, authentic crewneck...terrific colors! Men's $7.95. Wee $4.98. Prep $5.98.

McGREGOR
SPORTSWEAR
Stay boy-sized, boy-priced
McGregor-Doniger Inc., 352 5th Ave., New York 16, N. Y.   *T. M.

McGregor Sportswear, 1957   ▶ McGregor Sportswear, 19
▶ ▶ Van Heusen, 1950   ▶ ▶ ▶ Van Heusen Ties, 19

c'mon in ... the wearing's fine

Completely washable! They take to water like a mermaid. We're talking about
the new—and we mean *new!*—Van Gab sport shirts. *Gabardine* ... like you've n
seen! *Silky-smooth gabardine* ... with a new luxurious softness! *Finer-woven gab
... that wears and wears and wears! We've tailored this fine fabric with
famous Van Heusen magic sewmanship. Full-cut for action ... figure-tapered for
Shown here is famous California Lo-No model with exclusive two-way collar
... smart with or without a tie. Completely washable, stays size-right, color-fast.
See Van Gab gabardine in other smart models—$2.95 to $5.95

The ties: Van Heusen Washable Poplin in 100% Nylon, 18 solid-color Sportones ... $1.50 ea
Phillips-Jones Corp., New York 1. Makers of Van Heusen Shirts • Ties • Pajamas • Collars • Sport Sh

at those collars again! California Lo-No with "Fadeaway Collarband". Looks, fits right . . . with or without tie.   Season's biggest splash of color with 21 bright, new washable "Aquashades".

| et | Sea Clay | Shell Pink | Mermaid Mauve | Mist Grey | Tropi-Tan | Dune Tan | Ocean Blue | Sky Blue | Billow Blue | Pirate Gold | Sand Tan | Beach Beige | Deep Green | Briny Green | Gulf Green | Spray Green | Turtle Green | Sunglow Yellow | Oyster | Foam White |

Van Heusen
REG. T.M.

new Van Gab Sport Shirts . . . *Completely washable* . . . $4.95

for

closer

harm

new school of design in ties

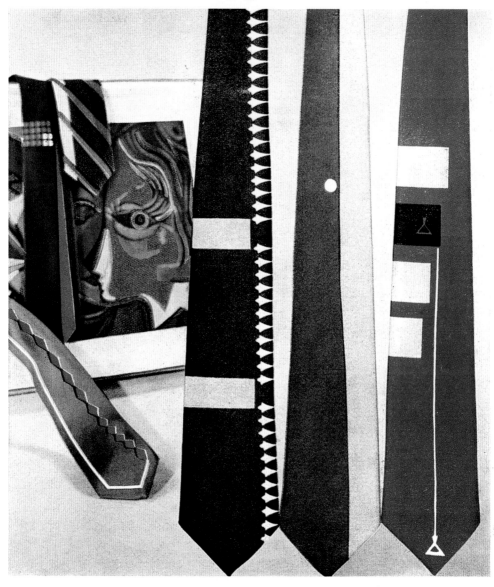

"side glances"

Manhattan combines the conservative and the unusual in a refreshing new note in printed acetate foulard neckwear. These new "Side Glance" ties offer distinctive designs—with the focus of interest on one side of the tie! In a wide array of color combinations—from bright to subdued.

Van Heusen Ties, 1950 ◀ *Manhattan Ties, 1953* ▶ *Manhattan Ties, 19*

HATS — As healthy as they're handsome

THE SOMBRERO — Originally introduced into Latin America by the Spaniards. Its name is taken from the word *sombra*, meaning shade. And a wonderful sun-shade it makes! It's cool, eye- and head-protecting, whether embroidered with colorful threads or decorated with jangling silver.

No MATTER WHERE YOU LIVE — South or North of the Border — the primary purpose of your hat is to *protect* you. In summer, its brim protects your eyes from aching glare; in winter, it protects your head from icy blasts. It guards your hair from the drying effects of the sun's rays, and keeps city soot out of your scalp. More things than sunstroke can happen to men who go bareheaded! Why ask for trouble when one of the handsomest pieces of apparel you can wear is a hat. Your dealer has handsome hats just suited to you. They are *right* for the occasion — wherever you go, or play, or work.

"Wear a Hat — It's as Healthy as It's Handsome!"

RICO TOMASO

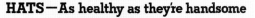

s, 1952

Hats, 1952

, 1952 ◄   Hats, 1952

Hats, 1952   ▶ Jockey Underwear, 1950   ▶▶ Jockey Underwear, 1950

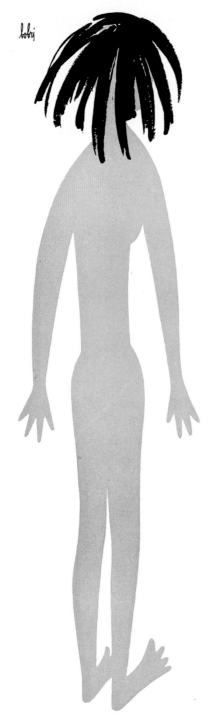

In 13000 BC smart women wore nothing.

In 1957 AD smart women wear nothing but **seamless** stockings by

Hanes

no seams to worry about

bur-mil **Cameo** stockings

...bring your costume color
right down to your toes...
lure your legs to new loveliness.
Ask for the new Cameo stocking
tints. Left to right, a sampling
of Cameo's coordinated
costume colors: Sea Grass,
Coral Reef, and Grey Haze.
$1.35 to $1.65 a pair. Full-fashioned
and seamless—stretch, too.

THE HUE IS THE CRY!

"*Cannon Nylons do something for my legs!*"

says the Cannon Go-Girl

She is a pleasure to paint – Your Cannon Go-Girl. Those Cannon Nylons do, indeed, do something for a girl's legs. I've noticed the smart new shades and pencil-fine profile they give.
— Varady

Go-Radiant—beige, with a dash of sunshine.

A second look? You rate it, every time, in your eye-catching Cannon Nylons.

For Cannon colors sing in soft autumn tones, keyed to fashion's newest spectrum.

And Cannon's *high-twist* thread sleeks your ankle, cleaves tight to your heel in a full-fashioned sheath.

Cannon Nylons wear well, too! No wispy one-day wonders, these.

Gals out in the whirl, out in the world, insist on Cannon Nylons.

Ask for them at your favorite neighborhood shop.

"on the legs that are on the go"

COPR. 1951. CANNON MILLS, INC.

CANNON MILLS, INC., NEW YORK, MAKERS OF CANNON SHEETS, TOWELS, BLANKETS, BEDSPREADS

CANNON

◄◄ *Hanes Stockings, 1957*　◄ *Cameo Stockings, 1958* ◄　　*Cannon Nylons, 1951*

Obviously, the lady doesn't know

Perma·lift's Magic Oval Pantie

CAN'T RIDE UP—EVER!

Obviously the uncomfortable young shopper on your right doesn't know that "Perma·lift's"* Magic Oval Pantie** Can't Ride Up—Ever! Tugging at a girdle is so awfully necessary with ordinary garments. But this can't happen to you when you wear a "Perma·lift" Magic Oval Pantie, for it's actually guaranteed to remain in place always. Be fitted today.

Pantie 3844—Power Net with front and back control. Only $5.95.
Bra 132—Fine cotton with Magic Insets. $2.50.

*Reg. U. S. Pat. Off. · A product of A. Stein & Company · Chicago—New York—Los Angeles **Pat. No. 2,705,801

Perma-Lift, 1957

247

WAKE UP
to Aunt Jemima Pancakes!

So light–So tender
they melt in your mouth!

No Wonder...

more women prefer Aunt Jemima
than all other brands <u>combined</u>!

Let your fork sink into the fluffy lightness of a stack of golden Aunt Jemima Pancakes. Ever see such fine, fluffy texture? Ever taste such melting tenderness? Now you know why homemakers everywhere choose these better pancakes. Treat your folks to America's favorites tomorrow morning!

AUNT JEMIMA
Pancakes and Waffles

AUNT JEMIMA
READY-MIX for PANCAKES

AUNT JEMIMA
READY-MIX for BUCKWHEATS

3 Piece Aunt Jemima SPICE SET!

For your most-used spices • Nutmeg, Cinnamon, Paprika

Nutmeg   Cinnamon   Paprika

TODAY! SEND
only 50c (in coin)
and the top from any
Aunt Jemima Ready-Mix Pkg.
● 4" high!
● Long-Wearing Plastic!
● Washable in Hot Water
MAIL TO: Aunt Jemima
Box D, Dept. 31
Chicago 77, Illinois

SPECIAL
OFFER!
Limited Time
Only!

◀ *Du Pont Cellophane, 1951*   *Aunt Jemima Pancakes & Waffles, 1950*

▶ *Puffin Biscuits, 19*

Post Alpha-Bits, 1958

Pillsbury Cinnamon Rolls, 1955

▶ Post Tens, 1955

8 A.M. and all's <u>swell</u>
when you get your choice

...ur choice of the world's choicest
...ls— in Post Tens!

...uldn't feel terrific at breakfast time—
...t wonderful Post Tens assortment to choose
...iss Freckle Face here leans toward
...uts—for more energy per spoonful than any
...real, cooked or cold! And whatever
..., all 7 famous Post Cereals are so nutritious,
...ous! Give *your* family a choice and change
...y of the week—this convenient Post Tens way!

For <u>goodness</u> sake – get Post Tens!

...ral Foods

AMAZING COFFEE DISCOVERY!

Not a powder! Not a grind! But millions of tiny "FLAVOR BUDS" of <u>real</u> coffee . . . ready to burst instantly into that famous MAXWELL HOUSE FLAVOR!

Utterly unlike old-style "instants" . . . just as quick but tastes so different!

In the famous Maxwell House kitchens this superb, roaster-fresh coffee is actually brewed for you. At the exact moment of perfection the water is removed by a special Maxwell House process—leaving the millions of miracle "Flavor Buds"!

100% Pure Coffee—No Fillers Added!

Just add hot water . . . and the bursting "Flavor Buds" flood your cup with coffee as delicious as the best you've ever brewed. One sip and you'll never go back to old ways!

Saves you money, too! The large economy-size jar saves up to 75¢, compared to three pounds of ground coffee!

See how the Flavor Buds "come to life" in your cup!

MAGNIFIED VIEW of new miracle "Flavor Buds" shows how utterly different they are from old-style powders and grinds.

THE INSTANT you add hot water, the "Flavor Buds" burst—releasing flood of rich, delicious Maxwell House flavor!

Reach for the jar with the stars on top!

A Product of General Foods

The only instant coffee with that **GOOD-TO-THE-LAST-DROP** flavor!

Maxwell House Coffee, 1953

▶ *Pan-American Coffee Bureau, 19*

THINK BETTER!...Minutes before air-time, newscaster Edward R. Murrow checks his script for CBS Television's *See It Now* — and takes a "Coffee-break"! Delicious, bracing coffee aids clear thinking. A cheerful cup can clear *your* mind for action, too. Whatever your job, keep yourself alert — give yourself a "Coffee-break"!

give yourself a "offee-break"!

WORK BETTER!...TV production is exacting work. That's why *See It Now's* director and cameraman break ... for coffee! Coffee's gentle stimulation makes hard work seem easier. Make a "Coffee-break" part of *your* working day.

FEEL BETTER!... The whole family enjoys Edward R. Murrow's thrilling TV show, and fragrant coffee adds the final touch. Relax often — with coffee "all around." With family, friends, or all by yourself — take a "Coffee-break"!

There's a welcome lift in every cup!

New! Chef Boy-Ar-Dee® Pizza Pie Mix

complete with mellow Italian-style cheese and Chef's incomparable Pizza Sauce!

Imagine — now you can serve this tantalizing Italian dish just as it's served in Naples — sizzling, savory, seasoned to perfection.

It's so easy with Chef Boy-Ar-Dee Pizza Pie Mix! Everything you need comes in one box — complete makings for tender, hearty crust ... zippy, tomato-rich sauce, ready to use ... even grated Italian-style cheese to sprinkle on top.

Baking time — only 15 to 20 minutes. Eating time — almost any time!

You'll love Chef Pizza, for example, as a tasty "fill-'em-up" lunch for the youngsters. And as the basis for a real Italian family dinner when you serve it with tossed salad, and fruit for dessert. (Each box makes 5 meal-size servings.)

But above all, try Chef Pizza for company snacks. Cut it in bite-size bits for appetizers. Serve in generous wedges for TV nibbling and late-evening party fare. Guests really gobble it up!

Remember to get a box — or two — tomorrow.

Chef Boy-Ar-Dee Pizza Mix, 1956

▶ *Van Camp's Spanish Rice, 19*

the joy of Good Eating

KE EATING CAKE—Van Camp's Tenderoni . . . as light, white, fluffy as an angel-food cake . . . for Tenderoni is the one and only macaroni product made with egg white. Cooks in only 7 minutes . . . needs no blanching . . . always tender . . . never doughy. Add salt and butter and enjoy . . . or serve with tomato sauce, meat balls, chicken, fish. Tenderoni helps give variety to your Lenten meals.

RICE AND EVERYTHING NICE... Van Camp's Spanish Rice . . . blended with tomatoes and peppers and other choice ingredients to give you the colorful, exciting dish that pleases all tastes. Ready to heat, eat, enjoy . . . to serve with shrimp . . . to stuff green peppers and bake. Make Van Camp's Spanish Rice your next adventure in good eating.

MACARONI PRODUCT
Van Camp's TENDERONI
MADE WITH EGG WHITE

Stokely's Finest
BROCCOLI
FROZEN FOODS

Enjoy the Garry Moore Show CBS-TV Network, every Thursday afternoon

Stokely-Van Camp's • TWO GREAT NAMES IN FOOD *that mean* QUICK MEALS *for you*

rach's Candy, 1957

Cracker Jack, 1955

Brach's Candy, 1958 ◄ *Brach's Candy, 1950*

► *Double Bubble Gum, 1953*

The candy with the hole ... *Still* only 5¢

THE TRADE-MARK "LIFE SAVERS" IDENTIFIES "THE CANDY WITH THE HOLE" MADE EXCLUSIVELY BY LIFE SAVERS CORP. IN THE UNITED STATES AND BY LIFE SAVERS LIMITED IN CANADA.

Life Savers Candy, 1953

▶ *Mounds Candy Bar, 19*

Treat Yourself to the Best-Liked
Coconut Candy in All-the World
MOUNDS

Enjoy Luscious, Snowy-White,
Tree-Ripened Coconut
With A Double-Thick,
Rich Chocolate Coating!

MOUNDS
PETER PAUL'S · DOUBLE BAR 10¢

TWICE AS MUCH!
TWICE AS GOOD!
TWICE AS FRESH!

IF YOU HAVEN'T yet discovered why Peter Paul's MOUNDS is far and away the world's most popular coconut candy, just open one of these tempting bars! Notice that fresh, inviting fragrance! Bite into that deep, double-thick covering of richly dark and luscious bittersweet chocolate . . . blended to our own exclusive recipe. And then savor fully that center of moist and tender, snowy-white coconut fresh from the finest groves in the Philippines! Every MOUNDS is *filled* with a wealth of this wonderful coconut! And every bar is specially wrapped to preserve its *home-kitchen freshness!*

● **Money can't buy** better candy than MOUNDS—the big *double*-bar for only a dime. Get MOUNDS! See why it's the world's best-loved coconut candy bar!

Masterpieces In Candy From The Kitchens Of
PETER PAUL

You'll Love ALMOND JOY
Peter Paul's Milk Chocolate-Coconut
Bar With Fine Roasted Almonds

Almond Joy

PETER PAUL, INC., NAUGATUCK, CONN.

"There's our man"—

You can always find the jolly Green Giant
ready to welcome you from the label

The biggest thing about the Green Giant is not his size. It's the feeling of confidence you get when you see his picture on a label.

That picture talks. It tells about peas that are still babies in tenderness. Tall, golden kernels of corn with summer in every mouthful. Grown with care such as no peas or corn ever had before. Then *picked and packed at the fleeting moment of perfect flavor.*

And all this just to make your mealtime life a little happier. Any wonder he's smiling?

GREEN GIANT PEAS BRAND | **NIBLETS** WHOLE KERNEL **CORN** BRAND

NIBLETS MEXICORN BRAND | **GREEN GIANT** CREAM STYLE **CORN**

Green Giant Company, headquarters, Le Sueur, Minnesota; Fine Foods of Canada, Ltd., Tecumseh, Ontario.
"Green Giant," "Del Maiz," "Niblets" and "Mexicorn" are trade-marks Reg. U.S. Pat. Off. GGCo. © GGCo.

Sealtest Ice Cream, 1956   Niblets, 1953

it's CHERRY PIE time

Where in all the world is there a flavor like fresh-made Cherry Pie? . . . spicy fragrance bubbling thru flaky light crust . . . meaty red cherries baked in the tart-sweet essence of their own juices—each taste a tingling experience—each slice a whole-souled token of summer's bounty. And this is the time to enjoy it . . . this is flavor's fiesta . . . this is summer's high holiday . . . *this* is Cherry Pie Time . . . whether you bake it, buy it or enjoy it at your favorite restaurant, now is the time to *revel* in America's best-loved dessert . . . luscious, tempting Cherry Pie!

AT YOUR GROCER'S—BAKER'S—FAVORITE RESTAURANT

it's Cherry Pie Time

NATIONAL RED CHERRY INSTITUTE

The National Red Cherry Institute, 332 S. Michigan Ave., Chicago, Ill., *representing cherry commissions, associations, growers and processors in Colorado, Michigan, New York, Ohio, Oregon, Pennsylvania, Utah, Washington, W. Virginia and Wisconsin.*

National Red Cherry Institute, 1950

All Desserts Become Glamorous with Reddi-wip

Just the touch of your finger turns gelatins, puddings, pies and cakes into party treats

No more dull, plain desserts! Millions of women have found that Reddi-wip turns every day's desserts into exciting, praise-winning treats.

Made with fresh, rich cream that whips itself automatically, Reddi-wip gives the festive touch to all your desserts, yet saves you work at the same time.

Add the glamorous touch of Reddi-wip to quick, easy-to-make gelatin and sliced bananas. See how instantly it becomes a dessert that looks as though it would take hours to prepare. See what Reddi-wip does to chocolate pie or chocolate pudding. Learn how it makes every dessert you serve more delicious—better looking.

Use Reddi-wip for a few days in your home and you will know why it has been welcomed by millions of American housewives in a manner not matched by any other product in recent years. It's so economical with dozens and dozens of servings in every can—and never any waste—that you can use it on all your desserts. Get Reddi-wip today from your milkman or grocer—keep it on hand in your refrigerator for daily use.

New! Easy way to frost cake! It's a great idea acclaimed by women from coast to coast. "Frost" each piece of cake with Reddi-wip when you serve it. Its fresh, delicate flavor brings a new glamor and deliciousness to chocolate, sponge, angel, pound and all your cakes. The same fresh, delicate taste that has made whipped cream cakes so popular! Try it the very next time you bake either ready-mixed or home-mixed cakes.

ASK FOR Reddi-wip FROM YOUR MILKMAN OR GROCER

Reddi-Wip, 1950

Only FLUFFO and PET Milk make it rich and colorful as Autumn itself . . .

Golden Harvest Pumpkin Pie

Golden Harvest Pumpkin Pie

FLUFFO'S GOLDEN FLAKY PIE CRUST (9-inch pan)

1½ cups sifted flour
½ teaspoon salt
⅓ cup Fluffo
3 tablespoons water

PET'S GOLDEN RICH PUMPKIN FILLING

FESTIVE NUT TOPPING (optional)

Fluffo and Pet Milk combine to bring you pumpkin pie so exciting it seems to capture the full richness and the golden colors of Autumn.

Fluffo can make pie crust this golden, flaky and tender. Only Pet Milk can make pumpkin filling this golden rich and creamy smooth—with just one egg. Now is the season . . . treat your family to Golden Harvest Pumpkin Pie.

Fluffo & Pet Milk, 1959 ▶ *Sealtest Ice Cream, 1955* ▶▶ *Coca-Cola, 195*

...enjoy food

Good things to eat
find happy companionship
in ice-cold Coca-Cola.
Here's refreshment,
flavorful and sparkling,
that steps up the enjoyment
of tasty things you like to serve.
Next time you shop,
remember to take *enough* home.

Coca-Cola

REG. U.S. PAT. OFF.

... and now
the *gift* for thirst

Drink

Coca-Cola

Always made from
tree-ripened
oranges!

Enjoy
true
fruit
flavor!

OTHER NEHI FLAVORS
NEHI GRAPE • NEHI LIME-LEMON
NEHI ROOT BEER • NEHI CHERRY
NEHI STRAWBERRY

NEHI ORANGE
(A SOFT DRINK)

BY THE MAKERS OF ROYAL CROWN COLA.

anada Dry Ginger Ale ◀   *Canada Dry Ginger Ale, 1950*

Nehi Orange Beverage, 1953

Industry
272

Symbolic of the newer chemicals for better living, this Hortonsphere looms up at an entrance to the Wyandotte Glycol plant. Its spherical shape withstands best the great pressures of stored, volatile liquids.

SPHERE OF INFLUENCE

The "sphere of influence" for glycols has spread so widely that, today, these useful chemicals are improving products in nearly every modern industry.

Their personality traits are many. Wyandotte Glycols *are hard to freeze, slow to boil* — so they find uses in *permanent* anti-freezes and coolants. These *versatile chemicals absorb moisture and evaporate slowly* — so they are superb humectants and softening agents for textiles, cellophane, smoking tobacco, inedible gelatin, glue, cork and paper. Glycols are also used in brake fluids, wood stains, perfumes — and as plasticizers for certain resins and as solvents for oils, dyes and other organic compounds.

In making Glycols, more than *half* the ingredients are chemicals which Wyandotte produces from limestone, coal and salt. Vast company-owned resources of these materials help assure dependable deliveries.

Other advantages to customers include Wyandotte's strategic Great Lakes location, for economical transportation by water, rail and truck . . . "know-ahead" research . . . an alert Technical Service Department . . . 60 years of experience. These have made Wyandotte one of the great names in chemicals.

Wyandotte Glycols may well improve your products and save you money. Our Sales Department will be glad to confer with you on their properties and uses.

Wyandotte
REG. U. S. PAT. OFF.

ORGANIC AND INORGANIC CHEMICALS • WYANDOTTE CHEMICALS CORPORATION • Wyandotte, Michigan • Offices in Principal Cities

Wyandotte Chemicals Corporation is one of the world's major producers of soda ash, caustic soda, bicarbonate of soda, chlorine, dry ice and calcium carbonate. Wyandotte produces glycols and related compounds, certain aromatic sulfonic acid derivatives and other organic intermediates. Wyandotte is also the world's largest manufacturer of specialized cleaning compounds for business and industry.

◀ *U. S. Steel & Univac   Wyandotte, 1950*

▶ *Aluminum from Canada, 1958*   ▶ ▶ *Al Stainless Steel, 19*

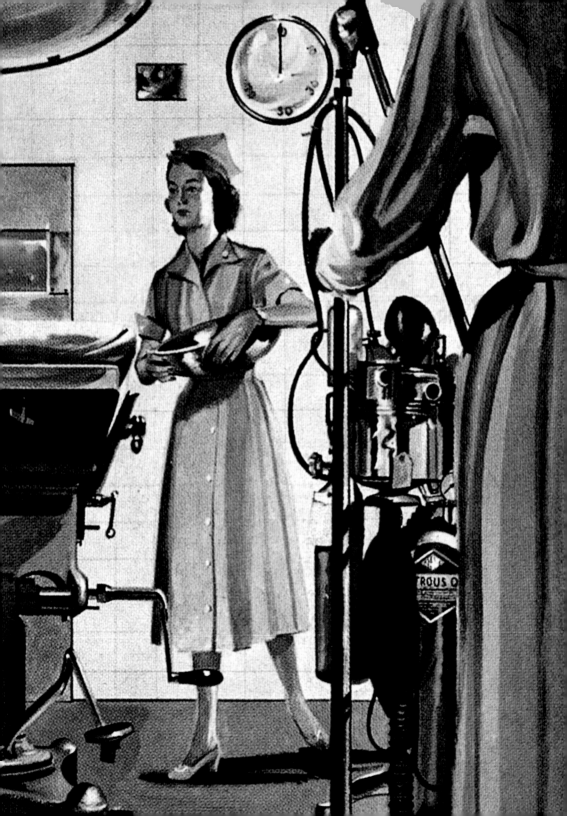

FAST FEEDING FOR THIRSTY FIGHTERS

Speeding "meal-time" for carrier planes was once a major problem for our Navy. Vital minutes were wasted because refueling hoses for aircraft were stiff, heavy and awkward to handle on a carrier's crowded flight deck. Furthermore, the hoses were deteriorating rapidly due to the destructive action of gasoline on the natural rubber.

A new kind of hose was indicated. Countless materials were tried without success until Hewitt-Robins Neoprene hose was tested aboard the carriers *Saratoga* and *Lexington* in 1932. The first *synthetic* rubber gasoline hose ever manufactured . . . it immediately proved successful. It was lightweight, flexible, tough, cut down refueling time drastically, and was completely resistant to the action of gasoline and oil.

The next step was obvious—Hewitt-Robins synthetic oil-resistant hose was a "natural" for the entire oil industry. Today, from oil well to service station, it has become an instinctive choice for handling liquid petroleum products.

Whatever you must handle—from gasoline to grout—you will find a Hewitt-Robins hose to meet your most particular needs. Hewitt-Robins has offices and distributors in all major cities.

Hewitt-Robins Synthetic Oil-Resistant Hose is specially designed to withstand deterioration and flaking from liquid petroleum products. It is lightweight, easy-to-handle . . . one of 1,000 types of specialized hose we manufacture.

HEWITT  ROBINS

Executive Offices: 370 Lexington Avenue, New York 17, N. Y.

HEWITT RUBBER DIVISION: Belting, hose and other industrial rubber products
ROBINS CONVEYORS DIVISION: Conveying, screening, sizing, processing and dewatering machinery
ROBINS ENGINEERS DIVISION: Designing and engineering of materials handling systems
HEWITT RESTFOAM DIVISION: Restfoam® mattresses, pillows and comfort-cushioning

Hewitt-Robins is participating in the management and financing of Kentucky Synthetic Rubber Corporation

◀ *Armstrong's Industrial Insulations, 1950   Hewitt Robins, 1951*

FIREWORKS AT 20 FATHOMS

Burning metal on the bottom with an oxy-hydrogen cutting torch has speeded up undersea salvage operations. For now the flaming finger of the torch slices through steel in a matter of minutes, where hack saws once took hours.

Making fire work under water calls for a special type of cutting torch, with three hose lines instead of two . . . one for oxygen, one for hydrogen, while a third carries high pressure air to blast water away from the cutting flame.

Hewitt-Robins Twin-Weld Hose is a natural for this operation. It makes hose handling easier—halves the danger of snagging and snarling, because Twin-Weld combines the oxygen and hydrogen lines into one integral hose unit.

Wherever hose must withstand unusual pressures or service, industry turns to Hewitt-Robins. We make over 1000 different types of rubber hose, natural and synthetic . . . a hose to meet every industrial need.

HEWITT  ROBINS

Executive Offices: Stamford, Connecticut

HEWITT RUBBER DIVISION: Belting, hose and other industrial rubber products
ROBINS CONVEYORS DIVISION: Conveying, screening, sizing, processing and dewatering machinery
ROBINS ENGINEERS DIVISION: Designing and engineering of materials handling systems
HEWITT RESTFOAM DIVISION: Restfoam® pillows and comfort-cushioning

Hewitt-Robins is participating in the management and financing of Kentucky Synthetic Rubber Corporation

Hewitt-Robins Twin-Weld® Hose is easily identified by the green oxygen line and the red hydrogen line. One stroke of a knife separates the connecting fin for quick and easy coupling to equipment.

Hewitt Robins, 1951

281

HOSE HARNESS
FOR THE IRON HORSE

Airpower replaced manpower for railroad braking with the adoption of the automatic air brake. But for almost 40 years after its invention by George Westinghouse in 1869, failures plagued air brake users.

Source of the trouble lay, not in the brake, but in the system's "life-line"— the coupling hoses that carried the airline from car to car. Existing hose couldn't stand the strain of constant flexing, sudden strong pressures, weathering and ballast scuffing.

Improving airline performance became a challenge to Hewitt-Robins. By investigating all the causes of coupling hose failures, we succeeded in designing the *first* hose that solved the problem. Hewitt-Robins Air Brake Hose made history . . . it was the first rubber product ever scientifically designed to meet a specific industrial need.

Developing better rubber products for industry to facilitate the handling of gases, fluids and solids has been the specialty of Hewitt-Robins for almost a century.

If you have a hose problem—or any bulk materials handling problem—have Hewitt-Robins solve it for you. Hewitt-Robins maintains offices and has distributors in all major cities.

For air brake coupling, or any other application . . . wherever hose is used in industry . . . Hewitt-Robins has designed over 1,000 types. You'll find one to meet your most exacting needs.

HEWITT 〈HR〉 ROBINS

Executive Offices: 370 Lexington Avenue, New York 17, N. Y.

HEWITT RUBBER DIVISION: Belting, hose and other industrial rubber products
ROBINS CONVEYORS DIVISION: Conveying, screening, sizing, processing and dewatering machinery
ROBINS ENGINEERS DIVISION: Designing and engineering of materials handling systems
HEWITT RESTFOAM DIVISION: Restfoam® mattresses, pillows and comfort-cushioning

Hewitt-Robins is participating in the management and financing of Kentucky Synthetic Rubber Corporation

Hewitt Robins, 1951

FINGERTIP ANSWER
TO A 70-TON PROBLEM

One touch of a button . . . and a 70-ton hopper car empties itself in as little as 90 seconds!

One touch of a button . . . and even hard-packed loads come free, leaving the car "broom clean"!

For coal, stone, ore, grain — *whatever bulk material you must unload* — the Hewitt-Robins Car Shakeout is the *modern* answer. You save time, money and labor by reducing demurrage charges . . . by cutting unloading crews from as many as twelve to as few as two, even one. You end damage to cars, danger to workmen . . . make a tedious, expensive operation quick, simple, safe.

Over *four hundred million tons* of free-flowing bulk materials have been moved "down the hopper" by Hewitt-Robins Car Shakeouts.

Like so many other notable advances in bulk materials handling, the Car Shakeout is a Hewitt-Robins "first". The *controlled vibration* that makes it so efficient is an old story to us; we've put precisely controlled vibration to work in a long line of time-tested equipment for screening, sizing, feeding, conveying, grading, purifying, dewatering or otherwise processing everything from bits to boulders . . . from pumice to pyrites.

If you have a screening problem . . . *whatever it is . . . why not make it ours?*

HEWITT (HR) ROBINS

Executive Offices: 370 Lexington Avenue, New York 17, N. Y.

HEWITT RUBBER DIVISION: Belting, hose and other industrial rubber products
ROBINS CONVEYORS DIVISION: Conveying, screening, sizing, processing and dewatering machinery
ROBINS ENGINEERS DIVISION: Designing and engineering of materials handling systems
HEWITT RESTFOAM DIVISION: Restfoam® mattresses, pillows and comfort-cushioning

Hewitt-Robins is participating in the management and financing of Kentucky Synthetic Rubber Corporation

THE HEWITT-ROBINS CAR SHAKEOUT is made in two models: Model GS, for plants unloading 15 cars or less daily, and Model HD for continuous, heavy-duty service.

Hewitt Robins, 1951

Merchandising's most modern methods work best in National's Long-Span Multiple Buildings

When the time came to pick a building design for suburban Cleveland's modern new Meadowbrook Mart, the most logical choice—from every standpoint—was a Stran-Steel Long-Span 50 Multiple building, 152 feet wide and 642 long.

First consideration was floor space, and the choice was strongly influenced by the Long-Span's provision of a maximum amount of unobstructed interior area—in the Mart's case, over 91,000 square feet ... enough for the more than 100 retail businesses that make it an outstanding service and shopping center.

Second was construction costs. Long-Spans go up rapidly and easily, so the

Mart's owners made appreciable savings in time and money by their choice. And finally, Long-Span was chosen because it easily lends itself to adaptation and modern treatment, as shown by the illustration of the Mart above.

The Long-Span Multiple, a product of the Stran-Steel division of Great Lakes Steel, fits into any size or any application—farm, industrial, or commercial—as readily as it did for the Meadowbrook Mart. Straight sturdy sidewalls and arch roof give a maximum amount of unobstructed space. Arch ribs and trusses of famous N-A-X High-Tensile Steel make for long life, strength and economy.

All-steel buildings are but one of the many special and standard National Steel products that serve many industries in many ways ... that make National Steel one of America's leading producers of steel.

NATIONAL STEEL CORPORATION
GRANT BUILDING · PITTSBURGH, PA.

SERVING AMERICA BY SERVING AMERICAN INDUSTRY

SEVEN GREAT DIVISIONS WELDED INTO ONE COMPLETE STEEL-MAKING STRUCTURE

National Steel, 1954

This is National Steel

Producing Quonsets–the "world's most useful buildings"–to help America swell production

Born at the Stran-Steel Division of Great Lakes Steel Corporation in the stress of World War II, the versatile Quonset has since proved itself the "world's most useful building" in many different fields of America's production and distribution.

On the farm, Quonsets are helping to increase livestock yields, save crops, preserve machinery. In commerce, everything from banks to bowling alleys—from service stations to super markets—are being housed in easy-to-adapt Quonsets! In industry, these all-steel structures are providing urgently needed factory and warehouse space with speed and economy.

National Steel products serve many industries in many ways. In addition to National's large output of standard steel products, its diversified operations provide special carbon steels for the canning industry; tin plate for the canning industry; zinc-coated steel for the home appliance industry; low-alloy sheets and fabricated steel flooring for the railroad and trucking industries; steel framing for the building industry.

All these products are National Steel from ore to customer. All are the result of the complete integration, the continual expansion that make National Steel one of America's steel production leaders.

NATIONAL STEEL CORPORATION
GRANT BUILDING · PITTSBURGH, PA.

SERVING AMERICA BY SERVING AMERICAN INDUSTRY

SEVEN GREAT DIVISIONS WELDED INTO ONE INTEGRATED STEEL-MAKING STRUCTURE

National Steel, 1952

▶ *Pittsburgh Plate Glass Company, 1958*

PPG AT THE SHOWPLACES OF AMERICA
Lambert Airport, St. Louis
Architects: Hellmuth, Yamasaki & Leinweber

SOARING ARCHES with acres of PPG glass give St. Louis one of the world's most modern airports. Colorful aircraft, trimmed and protected with PPG finishes, wing into Lambert Field . . . keep passengers comfortable with PPG fiber glass insulation.

PPG opens new horizons in this golden age for building things

We can build airports to express the beauty of flight because PPG glass comes in sizes, shapes and kinds to do it. We can build sleek airliners of aluminum because Columbia-Southern soda ash refines raw ore to make this light, wonder metal. We can build powerful engines that speed planes farther and faster because of today's high-octane fuels made with Columbia-Southern chemicals. Progress all around us—and practically everything we see and use keeps up to date with glass or paint made by PPG, or chemicals made by Columbia-Southern, subsidiary of PPG. PITTSBURGH PLATE GLASS COMPANY, Pittsburgh.

The Power Authority of the State of New York turns water pressure into electricity with the help of Shell Research.

Watts up at the St. Lawrence

SURGING through the world's second largest hydroelectric power plant, the St. Lawrence River will soon be producing 1.8 million kilowatts of low-cost electricity for the U. S. and Canada.

This electricity, coming from turbine generators embedded deep in the new St. Lawrence Power Dam, will serve farms, factories and homes. Only the most precise lubrication, however, will keep the 2,000,000-pound turbine rotors whirling trouble-free. A product of Shell Research was selected to help keep trouble away.

Shell Turbo® Oil was chosen for its ability to cool, resist rust and avoid foaming, plus its ability to protect bearings and shafts during the critical start-up period. These qualities assure economical operation for many years to come.

Developing premium lubricants that safeguard turbines over longer periods of time is another example of the way Shell Research works to assure you of better products, more for your money, wherever you see the Shell name and trademark.

Leaders in Industry rely on Shell Industrial Products

Shell Industrial Products, 1959

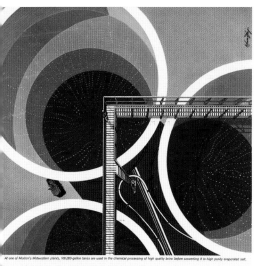

At one of Morton's Midwestern plants, 100,000-gallon tanks are used in the chemical processing of high quality brine before converting it to high purity evaporated salt.

Only Morton offers salt service to industry everywhere in America

Morton, the only nation-wide salt company, has salt sources, sales offices and warehouses from coast to coast. This means Morton can offer you complete salt service whether you have just one plant or several plants in different states.

To tailor-make salt for the many special needs of industry, Morton starts with high purity salt from one of its sources. With the aid of gigantic processing, refining and screening equipment, plus constant quality checks, Morton can produce and package salt to meet exacting specifications for any user—from mammoth canneries to small cheese companies.

Morton produces nearly 100 different grades of salt for industry. Morton delivers salt by boat, barge, truck and rail. This means you can get fast delivery on a bag to thousands of tons, anywhere in the country.

Morton sales representatives are backed by the services of their own ultra-modern salt research laboratory—the most complete laboratory of its kind in the world. This means you can get complete technical assistance on any problem relating to salt. This service help alone may be worth thousands of dollars to you every year.

▲ Salt Sources   ▲ Warehouses   ▲ Sales Offices

MORTON SALT COMPANY
INDUSTRIAL DIVISION
118 N. Wacker Drive, Chicago 6, Illinois, Telephone FR 6-1500

Morton Salt Company, 1959

Your letterhead is as much a part of your business personality as your receptionist. MEAD BOND for stationery and envelopes lends correspondence the authority and substance it deserves. Whatever the printing process, MEAD BOND assures a clear, flawless impression. For other office uses, there are MEAD MIMEO, MEAD DUPLICATOR, and MEAD LEDGER. Each type carries the distinctive Mead watermark. Each type is a specialist without peer.

Your printer or lithographer—and, behind him, America's leading paper merchants—knows that Mead Papers mean business. Ask for convincing evidence.

THE MEAD CORPORATION "Paper Makers to America"   **MEAD papers**
Sales Offices: The Mead Sales Co., 118 W. First St., Dayton 2 · New York · Chicago · Boston · Philadelphia · Atlanta

Mead Paper Co.

Take a page *from the official military report† on transistors...*

1 OUT OF 3 IS MADE BY PHILCO* EXCLUSIVELY

Transistors play a key role in the space age! Millions upon millions are earmarked for vital military applications. In the significant types, more one out of every three is designed and produced exclusively by Philco and its licensees... dramatic proof of Philco pioneering leadership in transistor research and development! The same ...ble performance demanded in critical military applications also makes ...co Transistors first choice for industrial and commercial use. To meet ... transistor needs... or for assistance in transistorizing your product ...consult Philco first.

PHILCO / LANSDALE TUBE DIVISION / LANSDALE, PENNSYLVANIA

PHILCO. TRANSISTOR CENTER U.S.A.

...al report of the Electronics Production Resources Agency of the Department of Defense, projecting military transistor requirements through 1961.   *and Philco licensees

...ilco, 1959

ELECTRONICS
is giant industry in the Philadelphia area, where you'll find such names as General Electric, Philco, RCA, Westinghouse and others. If electronics means business to you, you'll benefit from the "on-the-spot" contact provided by The Philadelphia National.

THE NUMBER ONE BANK IN PHILADELPHIA
—in the heart of the world's greatest industrial area

1803
150 YEARS OF BANKING SERVICE
1953

THE PHILADELPHIA NATIONAL BANK
Member Federal Deposit Insurance Corporation

The Philadelphia National Bank, 1953   ▶ *Western Electric, 1950*

GETTING CLOSER TO *Infinity!*

Businessmen, engineers, and scientists now are solving accounting and research problems which, a few years ago, would have been considered well-nigh infinite.

IBM Electronic Business Machines are making an important contribution to this progress. These machines accomplish once-overwhelming tasks with incredible speed and accuracy . . . freeing thousands of valuable minds for creative effort.

IBM ELECTRONIC BUSINESS MACHINES
International Business Machines

You are looking inside the world's most remarkable business machine . . . the IBM Electronic Calculator. It solves accounting and research problems faster than any other commercial calculator in general use.

GETTING YOUR ANSWERS

. . . at electronic speed !

IBM's vast engineering know-how is helping American business, industry and the Armed Forces get the answers . . . fast. Through its leadership in applying electronic principles to calculators and other types of punched card business machines, IBM has given greater speed, accuracy and economy to the nation's vital processes of calculating and accounting.

Already thousands of IBM Electronic Business Machines are in everyday use. We are continuing to manufacture them in quantity . . . as fast as quality production will permit.

 INTERNATIONAL BUSINESS MACHINES
590 MADISON AVENUE · NEW YORK 22, N.Y.

International Business Machines, 1952 ◄◄ *IBM, 1956* ◄ *IBM, 1951*

▶ *International Business Machines, 19*

PIERCING THE UNKNOWN

This IBM electronic tube assembly cuts through the unknown like a rocket through the stratosphere.

It probes the mysteries of the atom's core; predicts critical wing flutter of fast aircraft; traces paths of light through a lens system; calculates trajectories of guided missiles; plots the course of planets for the navigator.

It calculates payrolls, inventories, costs; points out savings of time and money.

These compact, pluggable units are the heart of IBM Electronic Calculators.

IBM
TRADE MARK

IBM Electronic Business Machines are vital defense weapons in the hands of our nation's industrial engineers and scientists.

INTERNATIONAL BUSINESS MACHINES

Now, your choice of color
...in the Royal Portable!

Sport coats, telephones, houses, refrigerators and now Royal Quiet De Luxe® Portable Typewriters give you the chance to express your personality in color.

And think what fun it's going to be to get better marks in school when you type your work on one of these gorgeous new Royals . . . the Standard typewriter in Portable size. Educators tell us that marks go up when work is typed. The work looks neater . . . is easier to read and grade. Spelling improves. Sentences become sharper and clearer.

You pay only $9.95 down. 18 months to pay the balance. Liberal trade-ins at your Royal Portable dealer's. *Remember: More students want Royal Portables than the next three makes combined.*

Based on a nationwide survey among more than 4000 high school students of both sexes living in 30 cities located in 22 states.

QUIET DE LUXE

ROYAL

Now in color—the new rugged **ROYAL**® portable

Royal Typewriter Company, *Division of Royal McBee Corporation*

MOST HONORED! MOST WANTED!
...and MOST FOR YOUR MONEY, TOO!

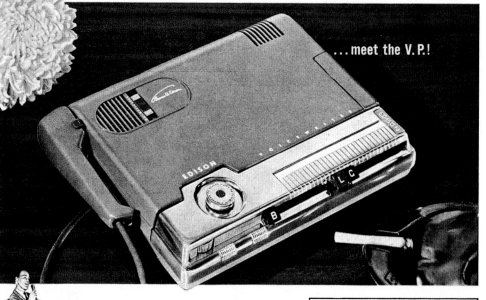

...meet the V.P.!

TINY BUT TOUGH! A dozen luxurious features have won the new V.P. EDISON VOICEWRITER its unmatched popularity, including: unique Master Control, automatic disc positioning, twice-as-accurate indexing. It's EDISON-engineered to take the most rugged daily desk use!

SMALLEST, LIGHTEST! Book-shape, book-size, the handsome V.P. is the most carryable instrument on the market! You can tuck it under your arm! And only the "Veep" permits *transcribing* as well as dictating ... a *complete* dictation service in one!

TWICE AS USEFUL! Cross-town or cross-country, the versatile V.P. slips right into your bag or briefcase ... goes home with you ... or on trips ... to meetings or conferences! It's a double-duty marvel, years ahead of the field ... yet priced *below* it!

V.P. Sweeps Engineering and Design Honors! The amazing EDISON V.P. has won the Audio Engineering Award, while its styling has won for famed designer Carl Otto the National Designers' Institute Medal. Make this prize-winning performer your *personal* dictating instrument!

FREE! 12-page full-color booklet "GET ACTION ON THE GO!" Just clip coupon to your letterhead and sign. Or phone local EDISON VOICEWRITER representative.

Thomas A. Edison
INCORPORATED

EDISON, 43 Lakeside Avenue, West Orange, N. J. O.K., send me "GET ACTION ON THE GO!"—no obligation.

NAME _____ TITLE _____

COMPANY _____

ADDRESS _____

CITY _____ ZONE _____ STATE _____

THE EDISON VOICEWRITER V.P.

YOU OWE IT TO YOUR BUSINESS
to LOOK AT *the* MARCHANT *Figurematic*

- EASY TO USE
- EASY TO OWN
- EASY ON YOUR TIME

Any way you *figure* — IT'S MARCHANT!

Your business, your office—whatever its size—can turn time into money with this new MARCHANT.

- The *Figurematic* is so simple to run that anyone in your office can use it swiftly and efficiently. Costly hours spent figuring by old-fashioned methods will change to extra hours of profitable, productive effort.

- Now, through our "pay-as-it-saves" plan you can *own* this moderate-priced MARCHANT *Figurematic* for less than the regular *rental* rate.

- Call the local MARCHANT MAN for a test run on your own work. You'll find that a *Figurematic* saves so much time that you can't afford to do without one.

MARCHANT
AMERICA'S FIRST
Calculators

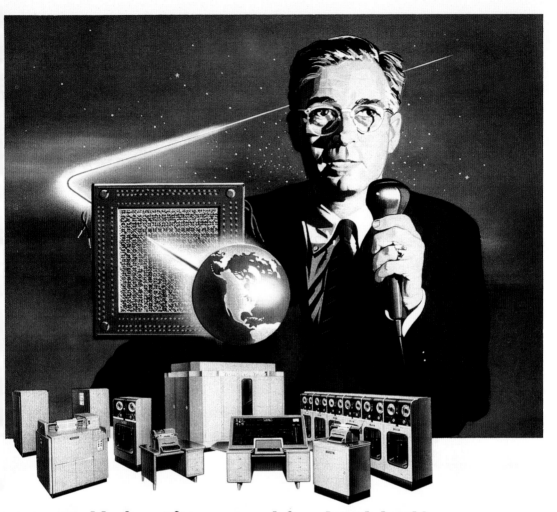

...now Univac's speed is doubled!

The famous Univac® of Remington Rand has widened still further its lead over other electronic business computing systems. Univac is still the *only* completely self-checked system ... the only one which can read, write, and compute simultaneously without extra equipment. And now, the Univac II adds to these superior features the speed of a magnetic-core memory.

The Remington Rand magnetic-core memory is more than a laboratory promise. It has been in actual customer use for over a year, passing all tests with flying colors in the first commercially available electronic computer to use core storage successfully.

The capacity of the internal memory of Univac has also been doubled, giving instantaneous access to 24,000 alphabetic or numeric characters. If needed, this can be even further increased to 120,000 characters.

Univac's external memory — magnetic tape — now has greater capacity, too, increasing input and output to 20,000 characters per second ... the equivalent of reading or writing every character on this page more than 1,000 times a minute.

These new Remington Rand developments can be incorporated into any existing Univac installation to double its speed of operation and to increase its economy still further.

ELECTRONIC COMPUTER DEPARTMENT *Remington Rand* ROOM 2205, 315 FOURTH AVENUE, NEW YORK 10, NEW YORK
DIVISION OF SPERRY RAND CORPORATION

◀ *National Adding Machine   Remington Rand & Univac, 1955*

Interiors
300

← RISOM

MILLER →

A NEW GROUP OF UPHOLSTERED WIRE CHAIRS DESIGNED BY CHARLES EAMES

FOR LOW-COST SEATING COMFORT IS NOW AVAILABLE FOR IMMEDIATE DELIVERY.

FRANK BROS. HAS THE COMPLETE LINE. A WIDE VARIETY OF MODELS

STARTING AT 25.00 INCLUDE THE TWO SIDE CHAIRS AS SHOWN.

ALL CHAIRS ARE AVAILABLE WITH FABRIC OR LEATHER UPHOLSTERY

WITH ONE PIECE OR TWO PIECE COVERS.

FRANK BROS

OPEN MONDAY & FRIDAY EVENINGS UNTIL 9:00

NO CHARGE FOR SHIPPING ANYWHERE IN THE UNITED STATES

◀ *Carroll Sagar & Associates, 1950*   *Frank Bros, 1952*   ▶ *Herman Miller, 1952*

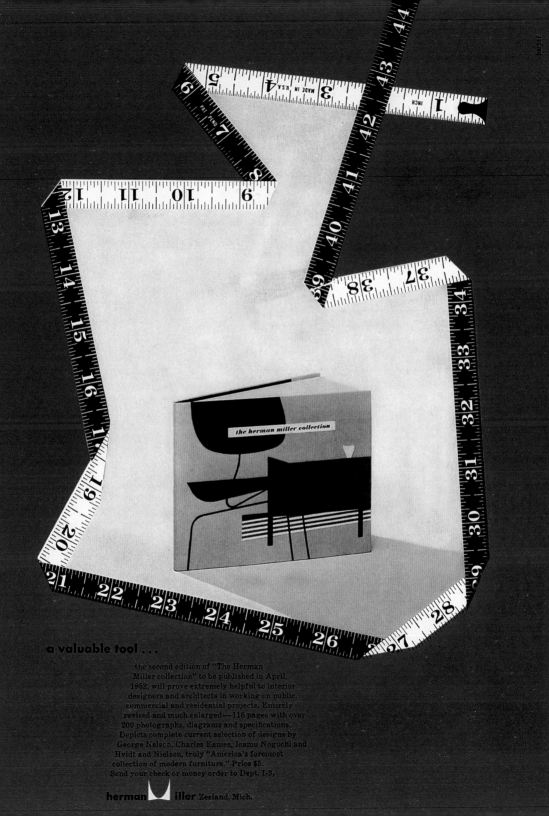

a valuable tool . . .

the second edition of "The Herman
Miller collection" to be published in April,
1952, will prove extremely helpful to interior
designers and architects in working on public,
commercial and residential projects. Entirely
revised and much enlarged—116 pages with over
200 photographs, diagrams and specifications.
Depicts complete current selection of designs by
George Nelson, Charles Eames, Isamu Noguchi and
Hvidt and Nielsen, truly "America's foremost
collection of modern furniture." Price $5.
Send your check or money order to Dept. I-3,

herman ⋈ **iller** Zeeland, Mich.

W ALL-ALUMINUM

EER FLUSH DOORS!

EQUALED

NDSOME, MODERN APPEARANCE

GED, INTEGRATED CONSTRUCTION

For Stores, Shops, Institutions, Schools, Hospitals, Hotels, Theatres, Restaurants, Apartment Buildings, Offices, Factories, etc.

Striking in their simplicity of styling and their lustrous alumilited finish, Kawneer All-Aluminum Flush Doors will add a unique and modern keynote to any interior or exterior. They combine good taste in design with the strong, eye-appeal of gracefully-fluted aluminum.

Their remarkable rigidity and durability are based on a new exclusive Kawneer method of construction (Patent Pending) which locks the two door faces to the interior framework, thus forming a rugged integral unit which assures long-term service and minimum maintenance.

Precision-made and correctly balanced, Kawneer Flush Doors will operate smoothly year after year. Their ease of operation is further increased by their unusual light weight—for example, the 3 foot by 7 foot size weighs only about 50 pounds without hardware.

In addition to the Standard Style shown at right above, Flush Doors can be ordered with one or more

lights of glass or louvers. Single-acting or double-acting doors are available as single units or in pairs. Hardware is installed at the factory to assure accurate fitting.

For detailed information, write The Kawneer Company, Dept. AA 49, 1105 North Front St., Niles, Mich., or Dept. AA 49, 930 Dwight Way, Berkeley, Cal.

THE
Kawneer
COMPANY
ARCHITECTURAL METAL PRODUCTS
Store Front Metals
Aluminum Roll-Type Awnings • Modern Entrances
Aluminum Facing Materials • Flush Doors

Good Reason for a Celebration!

You can hardly blame our rising young executive for declaring a night-on-the-town to celebrate his latest promotion. Just look at his handsome new office! And who could resist treating his wife to an after-hours preview ... especially when it includes a look at his new Executive Model *"Correlation"* Desk by Steel Age. This distinguished desk was designed to offer the utmost in efficiency and comfort to the man who makes achievement a habit.

There are *Correlation* models to meet virtually every desk need in your office. Each combines dynamic styling with complete adaptability to your changing space requirements. We urge you to call a Steel Age dealer for a demonstration of this exciting new concept in modern office furniture. *Corry-Jamestown Mfg. Corp., Corry, Pa.*

Have your secretary send for your copy of this interesting "Correlation" Brochure. Features full-color photographs of model offices. Write to Dept. C-3.

"*The Quality Choice of Modern Offices*"

Branch Offices: Atlanta • Boston • Chicago • Dallas • Detroit • New York • Oakland • Philadelphia • Seattle

◀ *The Kawneer Company, 1950*   Steel Age Office Furniture, 1957   ▶ *Yawman and Erbe Office Furniture, 19*

Herbert Matter

For natural beauty in your home

there's nothing in the world like WOOD

Beauty so stirring it invites your caress. Touch it! Enjoy the natural beauty of a living material . . . yours in unending variations of tones and textures. Only wood conveys such elegance. Only wood offers such *livability* . . . warmth and intimacy no other building material can hope to duplicate.

Inherently versatile, wood *belongs* indoors and out . . . responds to good design in any application. So rich, so *right*, you never tire of it. For has it not been said that a thing of beauty is a joy forever?

NATIONAL LUMBER MANUFACTURERS ASSOCIATION

nlma

wood
NATIONAL PROMOTION PROGRAM

Live, Work, Build Better with Wood

Consult your architect, building contractor or lumber dealer for more information on wood. And for your free copy of the colorful new 20 page booklet, "Livability Unlimited," write to WOOD, P. O. Box 1816, Washington 13, D. C.

National Lumber Manufacturers Association, 1959

▶ *Leather Industries of America, 195*

he Leather Look
afoot for Spring

The "Leather Look" is the look of beauty for spring! All across the country the "Leather Look" leads in fashion . . . and for good reason. Its lustrous tones and exciting textures infuse leather with the sparkle and spirit of spring. Remember, nature never makes two pieces of leather exactly alike. That's why leather can give you that touch of individuality. In shoes, clothes, handbags, gloves, belts, luggage — and a host of other fashions, leather means quality, value and a lasting look of beauty. You'll look smarter in leather! Join "The Leather Look" afoot for spring! *LEATHER INDUSTRIES OF AMERICA*

how (MOSAIC) tile helped make

THE PACESETTER HOUSE OF 1951

a spectacular success

The editors of "House Beautiful" have pioneered some unusually practical uses for Mosaic Tile in modern residences, where easier, more carefree living is the growing pattern.

The "House Beautiful" Pacesetter House of 1951, at Dobbs Ferry, New York.

Suntile, 1955 ◄   Mosaic Tile, 1951

How rayon makes your home say "Come on in!"

WHY IS IT that some homes have a wonderful "come-hither" look while others leave you cold?

It's a wide-open secret! Many a modern homemaker will point out that the lively, lovely, live-withable rayon draperies, and the new rayon decorative fabrics, make it easy for her to put warmth and charm into a house.

That's because rayon, being man-made, gives fabrics an endless variety of colors, textures, patterns and draping qualities such as grandma never dreamed of.

Today, rayon is wearing a special new feather in its cap—beautiful new rayon carpets. Homemakers everywhere are welcoming their brighter, crisper colors, their fresh new surface effects . . . and their astonishingly low prices. And where could you find a better place for rayon's utmost scorn for moths!

Look into these exquisite rayon fabrics, and the well-nigh magic rayon carpets, that years of Avisco rayon research have helped to make so useful.

American Viscose Corporation, 350 Fifth Avenue, New York 1, N. Y.

AMERICAN VISCOSE CORPORATION

WORLD'S LARGEST PRODUCER OF MAN-MADE FIBERS

Naugahyde, 1951 ◀ *American Viscose Corporation, 1952*

Duco® Enamel
Semi-Gloss
Jonquil Yellow

Duco Enamel
Spray Magic
Primrose Yellow

Flow Kote®
Wall Paint
Periwinkle Blue

Custom Color
Semi-Gloss
No. 1318

Look under "Paint" in the Classified Telephone Directory for your nearest Du Pont Paint Dealer

If you're painting something new, or renewing something old...

the beauty _lasts_ when you paint with the finest... DU PONT **paints**

REG. U.S. PAT OFF

Better Things for Better Living...*through Chemistry*

Armstrong's Linoleum, 1954 ◄   Du Pont, 1958

"Our bathroom is our beauty secret"

KOHLER SPRUCE GREEN has a clear, fresh beauty—lasting in appeal as Kohler fixtures and fittings are durable in use. Like all Kohler pastel shades it fits into varied decorative effects with individuality and charm.

Time-tested materials and careful workmanship guided by unexcelled engineering experience make Kohler plumbing a sound investment in health-protection and lasting satisfaction.

The smooth, lustrous Kohler enamel finish of the Cosmopolitan Bench Bath is glass-hard,

easy-to-clean—and free from effects of stress and strain because it's fused to a base of non-flexing iron, cast for rugged strength. The Gramercy vitreous china lavatory is typical of the beauty and practicality of Kohler design.

Kohler chromium-plated brass fittings work easily, with lasting efficiency. Be sure to specify them for all your Kohler fixtures. Consult your Kohler dealer on selections for bathroom, washroom, kitchen or laundry. Kohler Co., Kohler, Wisconsin. Established 1873.

TO HELP YOU PLAN
Send for our new free booklet C-2, showing practical arrangements of fixtures and fittings in modern settings. Illustrated in full color.

KOHLER OF KOHLER

PLUMBING FIXTURES • HEATING EQUIPMENT • ELECTRIC PLANTS • AIR-COOLED ENGINES

Kohler Plumbing Fixtures, 1950

▶ *Clay Tile, 195*

Travel
318

Panagra Airways, 1953

Pan American Airlines, 1959 ◀ American Airlines, 1951

American Airlines, 1950 ▶ American Airlines, 195

ONE MILLION

passengers have now flown the Boeing 707 jetliner!

These airlines have ordered 707 or shorter-range 720 jetliners: AIR FRANCE · AIR-INDIA INTERNATIONAL · AMERICAN AIRLINES · BRANIFF INTERNATIONAL AIRWAYS · BRITISH OVERSEAS AIRWAYS CORPORATION · CONTINENTAL AIR LINES · CUBANA DE AVIACION · IRISH AIR LINES · LUFTHANSA GERMAN AIRLINES · PAN AMERICAN WORLD AIRWAYS · QANTAS EMPIRE AIRWAYS SABENA BELGIAN WORLD AIRLINES · SOUTH AFRICAN AIRWAYS · TRANS WORLD AIRLINES · UNITED AIR LINES · VARIG AIRLINES OF BRAZIL · *Also the* MILITARY AIR TRANSPORT SERVIC

BOEING 707 and 720

Boeing, 1959

▶ *American Airlines, 19*

Only seven hours to brush up on your French

The superb Boeing 707 jet airliner goes into service first across the Atlantic, and within weeks across the United States.

You'll be delighted with the feeling of solid security you get from flight aboard this swift new skyliner. It begins the moment of take-off, as abundant, jet-smooth power lifts the 707 effortlessly to cruising altitude. You'll fly serenely through high, weatherless skies.

In just 60 minutes, you're almost 600 miles out of New York. In scarcely six hours you'll be trotting out your best French for the *douanier* at Paris.

The spacious cabin is peaceful and quiet, and completely free from vibration. There is only luxurious comfort, and a sense of exhilaration from the almost magical ease and smoothness of 707 flight.

Even if you're a veteran airline traveler you'll find flight in the 707 truly exciting—and secure. The 707 is the most thoroughly flight-tested aircraft ever to enter commercial service.

These airlines have ordered 707s or shorter-range 720s:
AIR FRANCE • AIR-INDIA INTERNATIONAL • AMERICAN AIRLINES
BRANIFF INTERNATIONAL AIRWAYS • BRITISH OVERSEAS
AIRWAYS CORPORATION • CONTINENTAL AIR LINES
CUBANA DE AVIACION • LUFTHANSA GERMAN AIRLINES
PAN AMERICAN WORLD AIRWAYS • QANTAS EMPIRE AIRWAYS
SABENA BELGIAN WORLD AIRLINES • SOUTH AFRICAN AIRWAYS
TRANS WORLD AIRLINES • UNITED AIR LINES • VARIG AIRLINES
OF BRAZIL • *Also the* MILITARY AIR TRANSPORT SERVICE

BOEING 707 and 720

Boeing, 1958

That first meal is the hardest
...but not for _You_!

Yฺou are looking at a meal in a mock-up. The Stewardess serving dinner is a _trainee_. She is going to BOAC's school in Heston, near London, for 12 weeks...before being allowed to serve her first meal in a BOAC aircraft.

At the moment, she is facing her most critical "passengers"...her own fellow Stewards and Stewardesses. They themselves are veterans. They know every move she should make in serving. They will catch her out in the slightest error.

Maybe now she's flustered by their scrutiny. Maybe she's taken aback by their questions in French or Italian. (She must know at least one extra language.)

Some day, all the strict training will be behind her. Some day, _she_ will have made a hundred crossings!

Some day, she, too, will be a veteran.

You will find her...when she serves _you_...competent, cheerful, courteous to a fault.

BOAC's British cabin-attendance is not indoctrinated in a day. You will not forget it in a long time!

No other airline can provide it.

Equipment: BOAC flies you in the most modern aircraft, including "DC-7C's", jet-prop "Britannias" and pure jet "Comet 4's".

Classes of Fares...BOAC tickets cost exactly the same as those of other scheduled airlines. Round-trip, New York to London, they are de Luxe $873, First Class $783, Tourist $567, Economy $453.60. (Subject to change after April 1st.)

Travel Agents' requests for your reservations are honored at all BOAC offices. They can give you travel and tour literature, timetables and answers to your individual questions.

B·O·A·C WORLD LEADER IN JET TRAVEL
BRITISH OVERSEAS AIRWAYS CORPORATION
Flights from New York, Boston, Chicago, Detroit, San Francisco, Montreal. Offices also in Atlanta, Dallas, Los Angeles, Miami, Philadelphia, Pittsburgh, Washington, Toronto, Vancouver, Winnipeg.

BOAC, 1959   ▶ _TWA, 1950_

Explore colorful, cosmopolitan San Francisco and Hollywood. Or simply loaf in the sun along beautiful Pacific shores, enjoying the extra time TWA gives you.

Your camera lens captures unbelievable colors in the glorious Southwest, where outdoor fun reigns in the wide-open spaces of dude ranches and resorts.

For wonderful fishing, fly TWA to Chicago and head North to the pine-forested lake country. There's camping, resort life, golfing, swimming and sailing.

Look for the new, the old, the smart and unique in New York — served by more than 25 TWA flights daily. It's a vacation full of memorable sights and experiences.

New England holds a trea... Americana, cool salt breeze... Cod sand dunes and sparkli... lakes nestled in the mounta...

Where in the world <u>can</u> you go on just 2 weeks' vacation?

Here's an easy way to measure your own new horizons along the HIGH ways of TWA.

You pick the places you'd *like* to go, then check the TWA time-map below.* Possibilities are TWA can save you so much travel time you actually *can* go . . . even with limited vacation time off! And TWA fares are surprisingly easy on your budget.

So forget the old, usual vacation haunts. This year, follow the TWA highway to the Great Southwest, to the east or west coast; to the mountains; to the seashores; to the Golden Gate or the Grand Canyon or the canyons of New York. You pick it—you measure it—you can make it, easily, probably in mere hours from where you are right now!

But perhaps your eyes are on the Old World . . . way, way overseas. How far is it by TWA? Look at the map again and see what a vast distance one single day's flight can cover. Yes, you *can* go to Paris on a two weeks' vacation. You can go to Switzerland; to Rome; to Cairo; to Lisbon; to Madrid. You can take your pick of these and many other famed holiday centers and resort lands along TWA's direct world routes and *still keep well within the practical time limits of a short vacation!*

If *you* have been dreaming about a certain trip, don't put it off this year due to a short vacation. Plan to use the speed of Skyliner travel to bridge the distance and make that dream come true. Your travel agent will be glad to help with all the answers to your trip questions. Or call TWA.

All flying times shown are approximate. Check your travel agent or TWA for exact schedules.

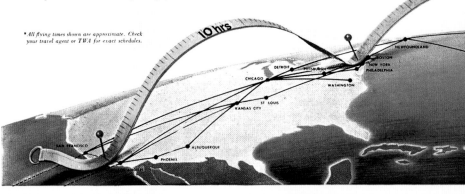

Ireland is a season of color-
d fun-filled events . . . from
nd fine racing to the famous
: Show in August.

For leisurely sight-seeing, try the quiet
lanes of provincial France. For gaiety and
sidewalk cafes—there's nothing like Paris!
16 TWA flights weekly from the U. S.

Like luxurious living? Then take a 300-
mph TWA Skyliner to the Mediterranean
area. You'll find the finest hotels and smart
casinos on the world-famous Riviera.

Motoring offers rich rewards in the
Swiss Alps, where breath-taking new
scenes await you at every turn. And car
rentals are reasonable in Europe.

Magnificent monuments and ancient art
masterpieces are everywhere in Rome,
scene of the Holy Year observances. Less
than a day from the U.S. by TWA.

f the pleasure on your vacation will be the few pleasant hours
ate, when you travel by world-proved 300-mph TWA Skyliner.
on as you board, the thoughtful TWA hostess sees that you're
rtably settled in a deep, reclining seat. She'll bring you maga-
playing cards, writing material . . . serve you delicious hot meals
it's time to eat. As you relax and rest, your dependable Sky-
speeds you to your destination in *hours* instead of days.

Across the U.S. and overseas . . .
you can depend on

TWA
TRANS WORLD AIRLINE
U.S.A. · EUROPE · AFRICA · ASIA

Ship almost anything anywhere by TWA Air
Cargo—fast, dependable, low-cost! For mail and
small packages, use air mail and air parcel post.

Leadership demands constant achievement

20 Distinguished World Airlines

have selected

THE CONSTELLATION & SUPER CONSTELLATION

On every continent of the world leading airlines fly the famous Constellation. Today more people fly over more oceans and continents on the Constellations of these great airlines than on *any other modern airplane.* It is also the leader on the most traveled route, the North Atlantic. This successful operation by international airlines established the Constellation's record for dependable performance—leading to the development of the new Super Constellation. today's finest transport airplane. Altogether 20 distinguished airlines have selected the Constellation and Super Constellation. Whenever or wherever you travel, insist on the dependable service of these airline leaders.° If there is no local airline office, see your travel agent. ° *Listed above on travel posters.*

LOCKHEED
AIRCRAFT CORPORATION · BURBANK, CALIFORNIA, AND MARIETTA, GEORGIA

◀ *Douglas Aircraft, 1953   Lockheed, 1955*

Sunshine U.S.A.

This is Florida—Sunshine, U.S.A.—where everything you do and every place you go are filled with glorious adventure.

This year take it *all* in—the brilliance of Florida's palm-fringed beaches and sun-warmed surf; the tingling excitement of landing that first, or *hundred*-and-first, big-game fish; the thrill of driving one down the middle of velvet-green fairway. This year discover for yourself the splendor of Florida's scenic landmarks; the glamour of its renowned spectator events; the romance of its nights under the stars. And this year see with your own eyes why so many millions agree, there's no place like Florida for sunny pleasure, healthful relaxation, and sheer good living.

Plan it today—your sparkling Winter with Sunshine in Florida—the vacation adventure you'll remember a lifetime.

Florida

MAIL THIS COUPON TODAY

STATE OF FLORIDA,
2201 COMMISSION BUILDING, TALLAHASSEE.

Please send at once new, free 48-page booklet in full color: "Florida, the Sunshine State."

Name_____

Street and No._____

City_____ Zone____ State____

Florida, 1950

▶ *TWA, 1953* ▶▶ *United Airlines, 1952*

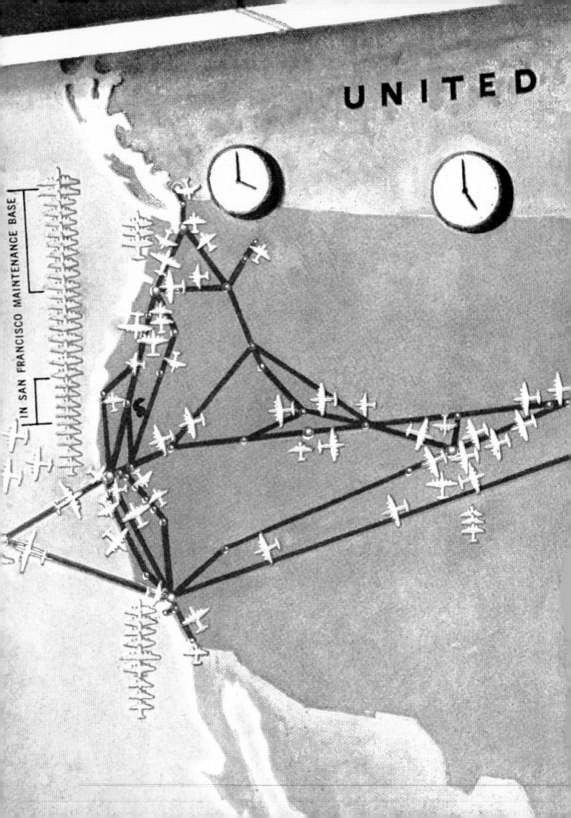

IN SAN FRANCISCO MAINTENANCE BASE

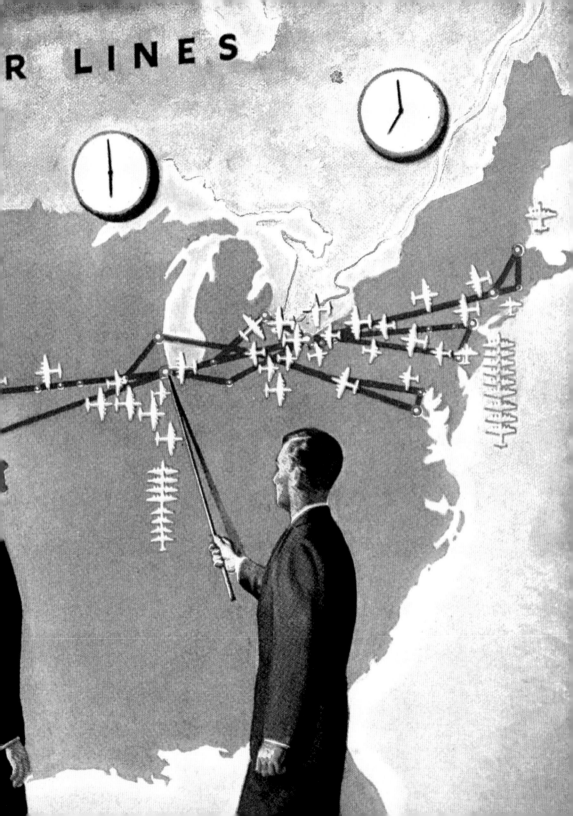

MOST COMFORTABLE WAY
TO GET THERE FAST

QUIET LUXURY TO MAKE THE TIME FLY – NEW SPEED TO SHORTEN THE DISTANCE

Largest, Roomiest
Airliner in the World

*Far Quieter for
Greater Comfort*

Wider Aisles & Seats

Larger Windows

Finest Air Conditioning

Restful 5-Cabin Privacy

Congenial
Starlight Lounge

Henry Dreyfuss Interiors

The Fastest
Constellation Ever Built

For all the speed, and quiet comfort, too, fly Super Constellations over every ocean and continent on these 20 leading airlines: AIR FRANCE • AIR-INDIA INTERNATIONAL
AVIANCA • CUBANA • DEUTSCHE LUFTHANSA
EASTERN AIR LINES • FLYING TIGER LINE • IBERIA
KLM • LAV • NORTHWEST ORIENT AIRLINES
PAKISTAN INTERNATIONAL • QANTAS
SEABOARD & WESTERN • SLICK AIRWAYS • TAP
THAI AIRWAYS • TRANS-CANADA AIR LINES
TWA–TRANS WORLD AIRLINES • VARIG

LOCKHEED SUPER CONSTELLATION

Look to Lockheed for Leadership

Lockheed, 1955

▶ *Lockheed, 1952*   ▶▶ *Lockheed, 1952*   ▶▶▶ *Cuba, 1950*

Lockheed sets the new world standard of Quality

New Super Constellation designed for non-stop international and over-ocean travel

Here is an airliner so different you'll be eager to fly on it again and again—fast, dependable, spacious and luxuriously beautiful—the world's finest airliner. Counseled by famous industrial designer Henry Dreyfuss, Lockheed has created completely new interior atmosphere for airliners catering to world travelers who appreciate non-stop schedules.

In service in 1953 between America and Europe on KLM, Air France and Trans-Canada Air Lines—will also span the world other oceans for Air India, AVIANCA, Braathens, Iberia, LAV, Pakistan International and Qantas. At your first opportunity insist on *Super Constellation* service.

LEADERSHIP
DEMANDS
CONSTANT
ACHIEVEMENT

Forward Cabin—Cabin No. 1 has fully reclining, adjustable chairs—deep cushioned, roomy, relaxing. As throughout the plane here is the comfort appreciated in non-stop travel.

Main Cabin—Cabin No. 2 with its wide aisle and broad ceiling afford unusual spaciousness. Beauty of line color matches that of the other cabin

The Super Constellation is the longest, largest, finest airliner ever built—with 4 superbly appointed passenger cabins, a luxurious lounge, galley and bar, 4 lavatories, crew's quarters, pilot's cabin—all air conditioned. Compartmentization creates a solid feeling of sturdiness never before achieved in any airliner.

Crew Quarters and Entrance — *Nº 1 Forward Cabin* — *Lavatories* — *Nº 2 Main C*

LOCKHEED
Super Constellation

Club Lounge — Cabin No. 3 is far the most unique, attractive and comfortable lounge designed for any airliner. Variety of seating allows privacy for 4 couples or mingling of groups.

No.3 Club Lounge   *No.4 Entrance and Galley*   *No.5 Rear Cabin*   *Lavatories*

...ey and Bar — Cabin No. 4 has ...e space for several attendants, ...ing quick service. Can be cur-...d off when used as entrance way.

Rear Cabin — Cabin No. 5 offers a full length view of the plane's beautiful interior with its mahogany paneling, modern lines and restful color harmony.

The Super Constellation is the most flexible airliner ever built. Converts in a few hours from first class accommodations to a high density tourist transport or partial cargo carrier.

LOCKHEED AIRCRAFT CORPORATION
BURBANK, CALIFORNIA, AND MARIETTA, GEORGIA

LOOK TO
LOCKHEED
FOR
LEADERSHIP

Light-hearted Latin gayety...vivid foreign charm—
in nearby

CUBA

"HOLIDAY ISLE OF THE TROPICS"

GETTING THERE IS HALF THE FUN

Crossing to Europe or cruising to faraway places . . .
don't miss the joy of going Cunard! Days and nights
of enchanted relaxation . . . laughter, music,
sparkling companionship . . . and the sheer wizardry of master chefs
. . . make your voyage a brilliant holiday in itself.

See your Cunard-authorized travel agent and . . . GO CUNARD

how to work up an appetite
for what's cooking in Caracas

Pirates had to eat, too, but they never had it so good as modern-day guests of the Hotel Tamanaco in Caracas, Venezuela, on the Ancient Spanish Main.

Whether you're licking your chops at the "groaning board" or "loafing it up" beside the sun-drenched swim-ming pool, you'll find yourself heir to the best of two worlds: the adventure of foreign travel, the comfort of American care.

From the food to the accommodations and entertainment, American atten-tion to detail tempers Latin imagina-tion. For that is what an Interconti-nental vacation holds for you: service and efficiency blended with traditions of hospitality that are centuries old.

So if you've been looking for a vaca-tion spot that's tailor-made for good times and good eating, the Hotel Tamanaco is your kind of place. Even without pirates, it's the most exciting place in Caracas.

Phone your travel agent or write Intercontinental Hotels, Chrysler Bldg., New York 17, N.Y. (If you prefer, call STillwell 6-5858 in New York.)

Elegant service — that's just one specialty of the house
at the fabulous Hotel Tamanaco in Caracas, Venezuela

INTERCONTINENTAL
HOTELS

The World's Largest Group of International Hotels

What's cooking?

A completely different holiday recipe – glorious sunshine, ever-changing scenery, amazing contrasts in breath-taking, adventurous South Africa! Make South Africa your travel adventure of a lifetime . . . see your Travel Agent or SATOUR for free and friendly information.

SATOUR

SOUTH AFRICA

SOUTH AFRICAN TOURIST CORPORATION
475 Fifth Avenue, New York 17, N. Y.

I would like to know more about a South African holiday.

NAME____________________

STREET____________________

CITY__________ZONE_____STATE__________

My Travel Agent is____________________

Step aboard the

Let us show you around the

You can see at **a glance it's different, because** it's so tall and sleek, but you won't realize how different—how quiet and smooth—until you **actually ride it**. **So step aboard** this new kind of all-coach train, and let us show you around.

Santa Fe

ew Hi-level train

er, quieter, smoother El Capitan

ee such roomy baggage racks? The porter keeps your baggage the lower level of your car, out of your way. And isn't it nice to be travel with *all* the luggage you need?

There's always a "show" going on. It's right outside your window. And when you go Hi-Level, you're up where you can see it all . . . as you relax in your stretch-out sleeper seat.

are window 2,224 miles long. No place like this dome lounge e sights—or just to relax over cool refreshments, conversation or of gin rummy.

Coffee-break in the Kachina Lounge. Make yourself comfortable in the quiet, intimate Kachina coffee shop in the lower lounge for a quick snack. Service from dawn to midnight.

ne Hi-Level, too. Feast your eyes on the scenery—and yourself famous Fred Harvey budget meals. With soft music and impeccable dinner becomes an event. Why not go *Hi-Level* your next trip?

$66 ¹²

(plus tax)
one way between
Chicago-Los Angeles,
including extra fare.
Lower with Family Fares.

*For reservations, consult
the nearest railroad or travel agent.*

New **HI-LEVEL**

El Capitan

CHICAGO-LOS ANGELES

There's always something going on in LAS VEGAS!

The Fabulous Resort Hotel Strip
Hotel LAST FRONTIER · FLAMINGO · EL RANCHO
THUNDERBIRD · DESERT INN · SAHARA

◄◄ *Santa Fe, 1957*   ◄ *North Carolina, 1951*   *Las Vegas, 1952*

Index

Imprint

To stay informed about upcoming TASCHEN titles,
please request our magazine at www.taschen.com
or write to TASCHEN, Hohenzollernring 53,
D–50672 Cologne, Germany, Fax: +49-221-254919.
We will be happy to send you a free copy of our
magazine which is filled with information about
all of our books.

© 2005 TASCHEN GmbH
Hohenzollernring 53, D–50672 Köln
www.taschen.com

Original edition: © 2001 Taschen GmbH
Art Direction & Design: Jim Heimann, L. A.
Digital Composition & Design:
Cindy Vance, Think Modern Design, L. A.
Cover Design: Sense/Net, Andy Disl and
Birgit Reber, Cologne
Production: Tina Ciborowius, Cologne
German translation: Stefan Barmann, Cologne
French translation: Simone Manceau, Paris
Spanish translation: Gemma Deza Guil
for LocTeam, S. L., Barcelona

Printed in China
ISBN 3–8228–4090–4